100 Ideas for Secondary Teachers

Supporting Students with Dyslexia

Gavin Reid and Shannon Green

Bloomsbury Education
An imprint of Bloomsbury Publishing Plc

50 Bedford Square   1385 Broadway
London   New York
WC1B 3DP   NY 10018
UK   USA

www.bloomsbury.com

Bloomsbury is a registered trade mark of Bloomsbury Publishing Plc

First published 2016

British Library Cataloguing-in-Publication Data
A catalogue record for this book is available from the British Library.

ISBN:
PB 9781472917904
ePub 9781472917911
ePDF 9781472917928

Library of Congress Cataloging-in-Publication Data
A catalog record for this book is available from the Library of Congress.

10 9 8 7 6 5 4 3 2 1

Typeset by Newgen Knowledge Works (P) Ltd., Chennai, India
Printed by CPI Group (UK) Ltd, Croydon, CR0 4YY

This book is produced using paper that is made from wood grown in
managed, sustainable forests. It is natural, renewable and recyclable. The
logging and manufacturing processes conform to the environmental
regulations of the country of origin.

To view more of our titles please visit www.bloomsbury.com

Contents

Acknowledgements

We wish to acknowledge the support and encouragement received from colleagues and friends - Dr. Sionah Lannen and Colin Lannen from the Red Rose School for children with Specific Learning Difficulties in the UK and Dr. Jennie Guise from Dysguise in the UK and Nick Guise for discussion and inspiration.

Shannon Green would particularly like to acknowledge Lois Lindsay from Vancouver BC for being her invaluable long-standing teacher and mentor.

We would also like to thank the publishing team at Bloomsbury for guiding us though this new edition of the book.

Gavin Reid and Shannon Green

Introduction

We are delighted to be able to offer this book to secondary teachers. While there is a great deal of material around on teaching younger children with dyslexia, there is much less available for secondary teachers. As we are both experienced in working with that age range of students we fully appreciate the challenges experienced by subject teachers in secondary schools.

We have therefore attempted to make this book as comprehensive as possible by including generic strategies and also subject-specific activities. We have endeavoured to incorporate explanations and a rationale for the ideas in this book, as we know that it will be used by subject teachers with less specific knowledge of dyslexia, as well as experienced practitioners. We have therefore made this book suitable for all working in secondary schools; to assist with this we have included an extended glossary at the end of the book.

This book is also intended to have international appeal; the strategies inside may be used by secondary school teachers in any country.

We sincerely hope you, and the students with dyslexia you teach, will benefit from this book.

Definition of Dyslexia

Dyslexia is a processing difference, often characterized by difficulties in literacy acquisition affecting reading, writing and spelling. It can also have an impact on cognitive processes such as memory, speed of processing, time management, co-ordination and automaticity. There may be visual and/or phonological challenges and there is usually some discrepancies in educational performances.

It is important to recognize the strengths, which can also form part of a dyslexic profile and they may need support to be able to utilise these strengths. There will invariably individual differences and individual variation and it is therefore important to consider individual learning preferences as well as the education and work context when planning and implementing intervention and accommodations (Reid, 2016).

How to use this book

This book includes quick, easy, practical ideas for you to dip in and out of, to support your pupils with dyslexia.

Each idea includes:

- A catchy title, easy to refer to and share with your colleagues.
- A quote from a teacher or pupil describing their experiences of the idea that follows or a problem they may have had that using the idea solves.
- A summary of the idea in bold, making it easy to flick through the book and identify an idea you want to use at a glance.
- A step-by-step guide to implementing the idea.

Each idea also includes one or more of the following:

Teaching tip	Taking it further	Bonus idea ★
Some extra advice on how or how not to run the activity or put the strategy into practice.	Ideas and advice for how to extend the idea or develop it further.	There are thirteen bonus ideas in this book that are extra exciting and extra original.

Share how you use these ideas in the classroom and find out what other teachers have done using **#100ideas**.

Study skills – making learning effective

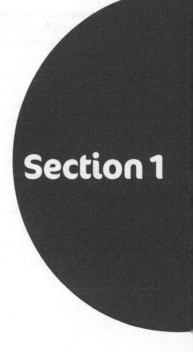

Section 1

Organisation – ten tips to stay on top

"Organisation is the key – it can make a 'big' task a 'small' task – this is a priority area for students with dyslexia."

More often than not students with dyslexia make progress with reading as they advance through secondary school. But organisational issues can impact on learning, with long-term effects.

Taking it further

Students can complete a more detailed weekly timetable, but this takes a lot of practice – you may want them to do one for after school only, and score out the school times, then they can eventually do the whole day. They can put the important tasks in a special colour.

Good organisation can help make learning more effective and also reduce stress and anxiety. Students with dyslexia need some support in this area. Organisation can take many forms, e.g. concrete organisation – materials, timetable, resources, appointments, etc. or cognitive organisation – arranging ideas, planning written work, retention of information, etc.

Ten tips to stay on top

1 Break a big task down into smaller pieces.
2 Set dates for working on smaller tasks related to the task.
3 Set a time frame – but remember you may read slowly and re-read to get the full meaning.
4 Do what's needed first – make a priority list.
5 Plan ahead – try to anticipate what you need to do next week, next month.
6 Give yourself time – listen to other students with dyslexia to keep things in proportion.
7 Outline the task before you start.
8 Personal timetabling – make your own schedule of how to use your time – as far as possible.
9 Combine short-term targets with long-term targets – identify what you need to deal with now and what you can leave until later.
10 Set yourself mini-goals – do not be too ambitious. Things always come together.

Memory – remember to remember

"I never assume I am going to remember something; I need to make a conscious effort to process the information and note it."

Memory challenges, whether for the working or long-term memory, are often a real barrier for students with dyslexia.

Students will need to develop their own memory strategies. It is a good idea to give them guidance on this rather than prescribe strategies, to allow them to develop strategies that are more meaningful to them and akin to their own learning styles. Go over the ten strategies below with the student and let them tell you how they can use them in different subjects – they could also record this in table form.

1 Chunking – breaking information up into small chunks.
2 Organising – arranging information in sequence and putting 'similar' information together – structuring.
3 Planning – arranging a timetable for study.
4 Visualising – imagining objects or characters and story lines – visual imagery.
5 Connecting – making connections between previous learning and new learning and between different curriculum subjects.
6 Retelling – putting a piece of information in their own words.
7 Repeating – practice at remembering information through rehearsal.
8 Re-enacting – the use of drama and activities – a song or poem to help them remember.
9 Understanding – they should be able to discuss and paraphrase the information.
10 Discussing – it is important to get them to ask questions as well as respond and talk.

Taking it further

This can lend itself to a mind map – discuss with the student a central image that can fit into the topic being studied. Then you can discuss the other factors – main factors and other factors – and plan the mind map. Mind mapping should incorporate in some way most of the ten points.

Studying for success – overcoming barriers

"Nothing comes easily – and effective study needs to be practised and the barriers overcome."

If there was any area we would identify as being crucial in supporting the student with dyslexia it is study skills, or rather learning skills.

The term itself – 'study skills' – can be a barrier for some students, filling them with anxiety.

It is a good idea to work with them to identify the barriers that might prevent them from studying successfully, and what they can do to overcome these barriers.

Look at the examples below, then students can present their own problems and solutions in table form.

1. Procrastination – Always putting off what needs to be done – often until too late!

Solution – Reduce the task to smaller, more achievable chunks and do these one at a time.

2. Anxiety – Do you find that you are being overwhelmed by the amount of work to be done?

Solution – Discuss this with someone – use priority lists, but with only two or three priorities. Even if you complete one priority item in a day, that would be an achievement – do not be too ambitious with priority lists.

3. Indecision – Difficulty focusing on one task? Constantly changing mind or thinking of the next task?

Solution – If it gets to this stage, put your list away; memorise the first item only! Do this one and you will get a sense of achievement, and this will encourage you to carry on with the next one.

4. Multiple distractions – Easily diverted from the task in hand – some distractions can include other interesting points you may discover when searching the Internet, and of course television, telephones and friends.

Solution – If you do come across interesting information, do not discard it or even study it, but cut it (or the link at least) and paste it into a file – labelled 'misc.' or 'spare information'. It is difficult to avoid distractions – in some ways you are wishing for distractions! So make up your mind that you will not be disturbed – you could put on headphones and listen to music while you are studying.

5. Frame of mind – It can be difficult to get started on a task – either because it is too daunting, or because it really is challenging for you.

Solution – It is important that before you start a task you know that you will succeed. You may want to spend a little time imagining the finished product or discussing it with a friend. That way you know you will do it! Start with an easier task; one you feel comfortable with. Then plan your work to allow for short breaks between study and give yourself time to socialise. Have a goal in mind – and it must be a worthwhile one for you!

6. Emergencies – We all experience the unexpected from time to time, and it is difficult to plan for this.

Solution – The secret is not to crowd your schedule or timetable too much – leave some slack. You never know when you will need it! Try to build in a buffer of time in your planning, for example to complete your written work a week beforehand to give you time to proofread.

Taking notes, keeping notes

"It is worthwhile spending time planning how to take notes."

Note taking is an art, and it needs to be practised.

Teaching tip

Ask students to write a one-sentence summary of their notes for each class period.

Filing and retrieving notes is also something that needs attention and can be extremely important for the secondary school student. A great deal of time can be wasted making too many notes and not being able to recognise or even understand them.

Notes should act as prompts when you are reading them over or revising. There are many different strategies for note taking, and essentially it is best for the individual student to find what suits them. However, students with dyslexia will need some help to do this. It is important to discuss this with the student first in order to obtain their learning preferences. You can then give them some guidance; the following strategy should be appropriate for most students with dyslexia.

The heading-prompt formula

Ask the student to divide a page into two columns: Heading and Prompt.

For example, headings and prompts might include 'The Crusades – battles, purpose, etc.', 'Richard the Lionheart – point to prove, army' and 'Constantinople – features, location, name of city today', etc.

Taking it further

After class, get the student to test their knowledge by covering up the right-hand side of the page, then reading the heading words, and trying to remember as much information as possible. Then they can check to see if they remembered correctly.

To do this activity the student needs to understand what they are listening to or reading; this is good practice and should be encouraged. What they miss in the notes they can find themselves later, but at least they will have the prompts.

Organise your mind

"I always encourage the student to develop active learning, not passive learning. There is no such thing as 'I will learn it later' – they won't – understanding is the key for effective note taking and study."

Information can be remembered more effectively if it is organised at the point of learning.

Dyslexic students are often concerned about getting the information down, and only try to understand and learn it later. When they go back to review the information they have often forgotten the context and may not be able to understand the information fully. It is more effective to try to get them to understand the information as they are writing it down. This requires organisational skills and practice at taking notes. Get the student to practise using the formula below.

Input – taking information in. The student needs to organise the information as they are taking it in by reading, listening or watching. They can put it into headings, subheadings or their own method of coding information – for example, bullet points or colour coding.

Cognition – processing or learning the information. The student puts the information into categories or groups of ideas. This will relate to what is already known about the new learning. At this stage they need to absorb the new information into their existing understanding of the topic that is being studied.

Output – reporting on the information. Now the student can prepare the information in some order for writing about it or for presenting it orally. Information will be recalled more effectively if it is organised – this is the key to a good note taking.

Taking it further

Get the student to keep a glossary of key words used for each topic. This is important, and can be very useful in developing comprehension and also for revision.

At the same time they should make up a list of abbreviations – again, this can help with reading fluency as it means the student will not have to stop reading and look up the meaning of the abbreviation. (See also Idea 7.)

Prepare a key task glossary

"I train students with dyslexia to use a glossary – it is worth the effort and it should be considered an effective learning habit."

Dyslexic students often get tasks and instructions confused, so providing them with a glossary is very helpful.

CALCULATE   Find a numerical answer.

COMPARE   Identify differences and similarities.

CONTRAST   Compare pieces of information, with a focus on the differences.

DEFINE   Give a precise description or meaning for something.

DESCRIBE   Provide a series of points in sentences that give an overview of the text or event.

DIAGRAM   Construct a graph, chart or drawing, or a visual portrayal of a piece of information.

DISCUSS   Display the points for and against a certain point and provide a conclusion.

EXPLAIN   Show that you understand a particular point, text or piece of information.

ILLUSTRATE   Use examples to explain a piece of information.

JUSTIFY   Provide a statement about why something happened or why you have a certain viewpoint.

LIST   Provide a number of items in a sequence.

OUTLINE   Present a general summary of an event or a text which will provide the key points.

PREDICT   Show the cause and effect of something or the likely outcome of an event.

PROVE   Show through a logical progression that something is true.

SUMMARISE   Provide a short outline of a text or piece of information.

Editing printed notes – steps to success

"A page of printed notes can be very daunting for the student with dyslexia."

It is very useful to receive printed notes from the teacher, but it can also be a bit overwhelming.

Notes from the teacher may not be sub-divided for ease of reading, and it is important that the student has the opportunity to edit these notes. It is a good exercise to be able to do this, as it can also help in their note taking from textbooks.

It is best to do this while the topic is still fresh – it should be done at the point of learning and not six months later.

The following suggestion for organising the information in notes may be useful:

1 Underline what you think are the key statements or the important concepts.
2 Use colour or other signal marks to indicate the importance of these points. If you use colour you can have a code – for example yellow = very important, blue = important, and so on.
3 Paraphrase the key points in your own words. Use the page at the back of the notes – if the notes are printed on both sides, take a fresh sheet of paper and tape it next to the page.
4 Write a key phrase for each paragraph. This does not need to be a long piece – maybe just four or five words, or fewer.
5 Finally, in your own words, take a page with two headings – information and implications –and complete this for the notes you have just edited.

Bonus Idea ★

Record and Play Back

You can get the students to record their edited notes and then play back to see if they still have the sense of the information.

Having it on tape is always useful as it can be uses on their iPod or phone.

Taking it further

The student could imagine they are an examiner marking an exam paper on this topic. They should write the questions they think they would ask. They can do this in pairs, and then discuss it with another pair.

Making full use of the library and the Internet

"For some students this is like an Aladdin's Cave, but they do not know what to look for first."

I think we all know how easy, yet how difficult, it can be to get the information we want from the Internet, or even the library. We have to understand the system in place and be able to access it.

This can be challenging for some students with dyslexia. They need clear instructions on how to access the information from the library and how the library catalogue works. It is best if this is done on a one-to-one basis and they try it out with supervision.

The Internet can be quite different, as it is very likely that they will be accessing this on their own. The main factor that determines whether the student gets the information they are looking for is being able to identify the key words to search for, or the questions to ask. If the student cannot do this then much time can be wasted, and they are likely to be distracted.

There is also a danger that the student will copy information from the Internet word by word. It is important that they do not do this; they must use the information from the Internet as a prompt, and not as the full answer.

Discuss with the student what they might want to access from the Internet. Try to get them to ask specific questions to help their planning.

Students should divide a page into three columns – 'Information', 'What does this mean?' and 'How can I use this?' – to record their findings as they search. It is a good idea to break up the searches into smaller parts so students can organise and remember why they thought a particular piece of information was necessary.

Managing time – the PPR technique

"It is important to appreciate that this does not come easily for students with dyslexia, yet it is vitally important and can make a significant difference to the quality of their studying."

Students with dyslexia can have difficulties with time management. At secondary school, students are encouraged to work more independently without too much teacher direction, so being aware of time and how to manage it is very important.

Prioritising

Get the student to consider all the tasks they need to do that week. Ask them to code them: one – very important; two – important; three – can be left until later. Then they should draw up three columns, with one for each category then rank each of the tasks, with the most urgent first. Then for each task they must estimate the length of time they need to spend on it in hours, half-days or days.

Planning

Now get the student to look at their timetable for that week and decide when they will tackle the urgent tasks, and insert them into the timetable.

Reflection

Reflection involves the student going through their work at the end of each week and asking questions such as:

- Did I reach my targets?
- Did I use my time efficiently?
- What factors distracted me or prevented me from using my time efficiently?
- How can I improve my time management skills?

Students should use their answers to improve their time management.

Taking it further

Get students to practise this at the weekend, using the activities they usually do on Saturday and Sunday.

Differentiation by resources

"This is without doubt a cost and time saving exercise."

All resources can be useful in some way, and they should be used to the maximum effect.

Taking it further

You can get staff to show how they might assess a student using differentiated techniques – for example poem, oral presentation, PowerPoint, portfolio, group activity.

It is useful to build up a bank of resources for students with dyslexia to complement your differentiated materials, and to share with other teachers.

Subject – ENGLISH

Resource/strategy – Using video or audio materials not as a 'short cut' but as a real alternative – good when first introduced to the theme.

How/why it is used – It can be multisensory and can provide the student with a clear overview before commencing reading.

Effects and benefits – Can help to clarify the background, concepts, ideas and the sequence of events.

Subject – MATHS

Resource/strategy – Knowledge and the use of learning styles.

How/why it is used – Using sequential/inchworm and holistic/grasshoppers analogy.

Effects and benefits – The sequential student can be accurate, but the student who would approach problems holistically may be more comfortable with mathematical concepts.

Subject – GENERAL SCIENCE

Resource/strategy – Labelled plan of the science laboratory and of the topic being taught.

How/why it is used – Mind maps can be helpful as they provide a visual plan of the room and the topic being studied – also helps with organisation.

Effects and benefits – Can be consistent with a global learning style, and the student does not have to read a lot to study and revise. It is also a personalised way of learning.

Subject – BIOLOGY

Resource/strategy – Abstract words and concepts such as homeostasis, ecosystem and respiration can be displayed visually.

How/why it is used – Can be provided in a notebook with visual illustrations or diagrams.

Effects and benefits – Associates the word with the visual representation. This can be reinforcing for the student with dyslexia.

Subject – MUSIC

Resource/strategy – Enlarging a normal-size score and using colour or coloured paper.

How/why it is used – Reading music involves sequencing and tracking skills, so you need to highlight the key aspects of the music sheet.

Effects and benefits – Makes reading music more accessible and less challenging.

Subject – PE

Resource/strategy – Provide a list of equipment required.

How/why it is used – This can be appended to a daily notebook or via email.

Effects and benefits – The student will not feel left out as they might if they forget equipment.

Subject – HISTORY

Resource/strategy – 'Print-free' debate; utilise strengths in oral discussion.

How/why it is used – This frees the student from having to read thoroughly before engaging in debate.

Effects and benefits – Can improve ability to question, infer, deduce, propose and evaluate.

Bonus Idea ★

Resourceful strategies – a whole staff approach

It is a good idea to build up 'resourceful strategies' that can be used across the school in every subject. Rather than re-invent the wheel it is a good idea to get a member of staff to coordinate with all departments and ask each to provide one strategy that can help students with dyslexia in their subject to then be collated and displayed for staff.

Differentiation by content

"Differentiation is the key to successful study. It opens up the topic for the student."

It is important to try to ensure that the learning outcomes are the same for all students, including those with dyslexia.

For example, the learning outcome for Biology may be to describe all the features of a frog, but the **content** of the activity sheet can be at different levels in terms of the ideas, concepts, use of visuals and vocabulary.

The text – You must consider points such as vocabulary, length of sentences, clarity of phrases used, the structure and style of the text, and the avoidance of ambiguous sentences.

The use of visuals – This helps clarify the content, and as a general rule more visuals should make the content simpler and clearer.

The concepts – It is important that the ideas and the concepts contained in the text are accessible.

Knowledge base – It is best if you know the student's previous knowledge and understanding. Start with a recapping paragraph identifying the key points.

Following is an example showing three different levels of differentiation.

Level 1 (Difficult)

The frog has relatively smooth skin, which varies in colour from olive green and yellow to dark brown.

Level 2 (Less difficult)

The frog – Show an annotated picture of a frog.

Skin – Smooth skin.

Colour – Olive green, yellow and dark brown.

Key words – This should be provided so students will be able to identify the key elements in the text.

Self-knowledge/study plan

"It is important for the student to realise that they will need to do this themselves and that the teacher will not always be there to support them."

Try to promote independence as far as possible. Self-knowledge can be the key to effective study skills.

Students with dyslexia can too easily become 'bogged down' in the mechanics of a task, and unaware of how they actually carried it out. It is important to help them recognise the learning processes they have been using. This can also relate to the learning environment, and they should be encouraged to develop an awareness of the environments they are best suited to.

To help the student with dyslexia develop and become aware of themselves as a learner, try the following exercise with them.

- Make a list of the things around you that can distract you when learning.
- List those aspects that are the most distracting.
- Indicate why you think these aspects are distracting.
- Is it possible to avoid these factors?
- Show how they can be avoided.
- Now list those aspects that help you concentrate better when learning.
- Why do you think they help you concentrate better?
- Is it the same for every type of learning, or does it depend on what type of activity you are doing?
- Now make a self-study plan from your responses above that will show your learning preferences. Fill in a chart with four column headings: Activity, What helps concentration, Distractions, Action.

Taking it further

Get students to try the following metacognitive cycle, which can promote independent learning. First guide them through this cycle using a piece of information they are familiar with. Eventually they should be able to do this themselves.

The cycle involves:

- Self-questioning – 'Why, what, where, how?'
- Self-clarifying – 'I see, but what about this?'
- Self-understanding – 'Right, I get it now.'
- Self-connecting – 'I did something like this last week.'
- Self-directing – 'OK, I know what to do know.'
- Self monitoring – 'Maybe I should do this now – that does not seem to be correct.'
- Self-assessing – 'So far so good.'

English

Section 2

Reading fluency

"Reading is tough, because in order to understand what they read, students have to be able to read fluently."

Being able to read text fluently and accurately helps to develop comprehension, but dyslexic children often have difficulty with this.

Taking it further

Present the new words that students will experience in their reading. Have the students look the words up in the dictionary and then write phrases using the new words in context. They can be given an opportunity to discuss the new word in each phrase, and can then turn the phrases into sentences. (Orally or written.) This process can also be done in reverse, where students are given sentences and asked to break them into phrases, then have them read the phrases aloud. Re-read until the phrases can be read fluently with voiced expression.

Reading is often a word-by-word struggle with little voiced expression or comprehension. There is no quick fix to reading fluency; students need a direct approach with support, encouragement and a lot of practice. Students need to read and re-read decodable text so that they understand that reading should sound like talking.

Activities

Reading in phrases is a good way to practise reading smoothly, accurately and with comprehension.

- Begin by presenting phrases for the student to read. You can take phrases from their reading or make up fun, creative ones. The goal is to have the student understand that words are related to each other in order to either add more information or provide the crucial information in a sentence.
- Ask the students to read the phrases, then turn the phrase, text side down, and say what they have read. This can be done as drill reading, using the same phrases until they can be read smoothly, accurately and quickly.
- Practice is key to reading fluency, so have the student read and re-read.

Skim reading for comprehension

"Learning to skim through a chapter has helped me feel less dread about learning. I can now skim for clues on what a chapter is about so I have an overview before I even start reading."

Skim reading is useful for surveying a text to get a general idea of what it is about. This can be an important part of comprehension for dyslexic learners, as they often need the big picture in order to understand the parts.

Students learn to pass over the text, looking for essential information and skipping over the insignificant or less important details.

It can be useful to pay attention to how the text is organised. In textbooks, the content is often organised through chapter headings and subheadings. You can therefore get a good idea of the overall content of a text by reading these first.

The idea is to provide opportunities for students to absorb the main ideas of a text, and then later cement them by reading the contents with intent. Skimming gives the reader a sense of topic, purpose and organisation, and of the ease or difficulty of the text.

Taking it further

Give students a reason to skim through a chapter so they are interacting with the text.

For example: Now–Next–Later

1. Have students skim through a chapter of a textbook, looking for titles, headings and subheadings.
2. Next, have them try to get some idea of what the text is about by taking each title, heading and subheading and turning them into questions.
3. Later, when the students are reading the content more carefully, have them answer the questions they formulated while skimming.

Scanning for accuracy

"Learning to scan was challenging because I was used to reading everything. Giving myself permission to scan was an important step towards learning the skill."

Scanning is a technique you use when you are examining a text for specific information. In most cases you know what you are looking for, and so you are concentrating on finding a particular answer by looking for key words or ideas.

Taking it further

When doing a research project, have students scan websites, indexes of resource books and reference materials intentionally by using key words. This can provide information about whether the material will be useful and, if so, the pages where the information can be found.

Scanning involves moving your eyes over a text very quickly, seeking specific words or phrases. This skill can be very challenging for a learner with dyslexia because in order for it to be effective they need to know what to look for, be able to move through a text quickly, comprehend what they are reading and understand how the information is structured. Therefore, it can be helpful to provide a purpose so the student knows what to scan for.

There are many reasons to scan, and using everyday material may be a good way to practise the skill. For example, look up sports scores in a newspaper, scan a cable guide for a favourite TV show, or look up a friend's phone number or a word in a dictionary.

Scanning adds another dimension to reading, and the more practice given to this skill, the more effective a student will become.

Short sentences and visuals

"After I write something for the students I always look how I can shorten the sentences – I would rather use two or three short sentences with a visual than a longer sentence."

It is important to keep sentences short and vocabulary simple.

To do this you will need to have some knowledge of the students' level of reading and vocabulary. It is worthwhile doing this first, as for some students you may need to make an individualised note.

For example, you might say, 'The Spanish Armada was a powerful maritime force, and other countries feared the speed of the ships and the skills of the sailors.' Although that is not really a long sentence, it may be too long for students with dyslexia. There are three concepts/ideas in this sentence – *the force of the Armada*, *the speed of the ships* and *the skills of the sailors*. The sentence could therefore have been presented as follows:

The Spanish Armada was a powerful maritime force.

Most of the countries nearby feared the speed of the Armada ships.

The sailors of the Spanish Armada were well trained and well equipped.

It is important that sentences such as those above are supported by visuals. The student may rely heavily on visuals for understanding the content and concepts, as they can make the task more accessible. Highlight the key words with colour or bold text and, where possible, pictures. So, for example, the above sentences can be made easier for dyslexic students by inserting pictures after each one.

Bonus Idea ★

One Idea per sentence
Get the student to identify a look at a recent essay or piece of written work then ask them to write the one idea or main point of each sentence. If it has more than one idea or point they should then re-write it into different sentences.

Taking it further

You could get the student themselves to show how text can be simplified – get them to go over a piece of text and ask them how it could be made easier for them to read. This can be quite revealing.

21

Topic-specific vocabulary

"Vocabulary that is specific to a subject or topic should be thought about at the planning stage and presented to the dyslexic student at the time of learning."

It is a good idea to display a chart with topic-specific vocabulary on the wall.

Different colours can be used for different topics. You can also get the dyslexic student to make up their own subject vocabulary and develop this as they meet new topic-specific words. It might be advisable also to indicate a brief meaning beside each word, as this can also help with retention. Some topic-specific vocabulary is shown below.

Taking it further

You can make this a class task, and do a poster with the different words; one for each subject or topic. Get the students to work in groups and each group to do one poster. Involve a teacher from the relevant subject and make it a cross-curricular activity.

History
Epoch
Dynasty
Revolution

Geography
Climate
Environment
Terrain

Chemistry
Compound
Experiment
Mutation

Biology
Cell
Physiological
Stem

English
Literature
Metaphor
Syntax

Mathematics
Calculate
Formulae
Fraction

Art
Easel
Sketch
Texture

Physical Education
Words used in specific sports such as: ace, dugout, free kick, putt

Music
Notes
Orchestra
Score
Sheet

Modern Languages
Accent
Culture
Customs
Parts of speech

Tackling a novel study

"Providing the steps so students know what to do can make the daunting task of a novel study more manageable."

Novel studies can be daunting for students with dyslexia. It is essential to break the work down into manageable chunks so that students will understand the task and know the sequence in which to complete it.

Planning is a skill that many learners struggle to develop. Therefore scaffolding is an excellent technique to use, providing an opportunity for teachers and students to work together so the student knows what to do, when to do it and why. The key element is for the teacher to show how to tackle the process and to reveal the thinking that goes with it.

The first step is to create a sequence in the form of a checklist. It will look different for each assignment, but may include all or some of the following:

- Read the text as a whole for comprehension. Use colour-coded notes to mark important or confusing parts or strong, supporting sections that may be useful for interpretation later.
- Does it make sense as a whole?
- Do I need to re-read? Ask questions? Look things up? Does anything need to be clarified?
- Create a sequence of events outlining the beginning, middle and end. You may need to re-read sections in order to complete this.
- It may be helpful to do this for each chapter.
- You may use a diagram to highlight the essential elements such as beginning, rising action, climax, falling action and resolution.
- Interpretation – fill in the bits that are missing.
- Theme.
- Character analysis.
- Plot.

Taking it further

Finding quotations to reinforce points is a crucial but challenging part of the process. Working in groups can be helpful and can eliminate stress. Choose a point to be made about the novel and then ask for several quotations to support the novel. You can host a debate about who has the stronger quotation to support the point, and why. The modelling of selecting quotations as well as the discussion will help the student with dyslexia understand the task and will foster the idea that there are valid alternative interpretations.

Organise your English notes

"Every time I hear a student say 'I took a note but can't find it now' I say to myself – I need to help them!"

A great deal of effort goes into writing notes, and it is crucially important that these are organised and can be retrieved.

Taking it further

Decorate your folder (yes!) – but try to make it appropriate – no guitars unless it is music; no football unless it is PE...being appropriate with your cover can help you find the right folder at the right time!

For students with dyslexia, the notes are often misplaced or sometimes lost altogether. Here are some golden rules for organising notes.

- **Index of notes** – Know what you have written notes on, what is the source of the notes and the date taken, and other important details about the notes. Keep an index, and keep it up to date.
- **Why take notes** – As soon as you set about writing any kind of notes you need to have a purpose – what are you looking for; what questions are in your mind?
- **File by topic, not date** – Have an index card for each topic. This makes it easier to file by topic – it is worth taking the time to do this.
- **Use a loose-leaf binder file** – This makes it easier to add notes and other pieces of information to the topic.
- **Label the binder file** – Make sure the binder file is labelled so that you can tell at a glance what the file contains.
- **Timetable and calendar** – Stick a timetable and events calendar in the inside cover of your binder. You should do this for every binder so you do not have to scramble looking for your timetable.
- **Glossary** – Keep a glossary or a timeline in history and insert this at the back of your file under a separate heading. This makes it easier to locate and add things to. (You may also want to add a personal spelling list of the words you find challenging.)

Acting the part

"We always dramatise the play we are doing, as it is very multisensory but also uses other skills."

Students with dyslexia can find novels and plays really exciting and thought provoking.

It is significant that many students with dyslexia opt to study English Literature at university. They can be very insightful in this area but often have difficulty remembering characters and the details. Students could look at some of the strategies used by professional actors who are dyslexic to inspire them.

For example actress Kara Tointon, when learning her lines, uses green-tinted glasses to soften the look of the words on scripts. She said: 'It takes me a long time, but once I've learned lines they are in my mind for life.'

Orlando Bloom talks about the challenge of line-learning and how he has 'learned to live with it' and also learned to overcome it. Keira Knightley says she 'worked hard to get the better of it and by the time [she] got to secondary school, it was much better'.

Former *EastEnders* actress Carol Harrison recognises that: '... having dyslexia has made me a better actor because instead of just saying the words, [I] have to feel them very, very deeply, take them inside of [my]self, process them and bring them out again.'

When you are reading a play or trying to memorise words, move around the room. Look at the props in the room and, when you are rehearsing the words, focus on a prop (as long as the same prop will be on stage when you are acting in front of the audience). This memory training method requires practice but can be very effective.

Taking it further

You could try to generalise this strategy by walking outside if you are trying to remember lines, and looking for images that may prompt the line you are remembering. For example, when walking along the beach or shore conjure up that image later, and the lines you are trying to remember should flow back.

Preparing and answering essay questions

"I always spend a great deal of time on this, as students are going to be using essay writing skills for some time."

Students with dyslexia can have difficulty planning, preparing and writing essay questions. As well as practice they need some guidance in the sequence they should follow.

Quite often they have difficulty in making a start to an essay, and they may need some prompts on what to do next.

Provide a series of headings with directions and questions that can prompt them on what they should be doing, and when.

Preparation

- Examine the question, topic or issue.
- Ask yourself what the question means.
- Write down what you think the question is asking.
- What do you already know about the topic?
- What do you still have to find out?
- What is your answer to the question?
- What detail would support your answer?

Gathering

- What sort of information do you need?
- Where will you find it?
- What are the key points?
- Keep a record of where you obtained information.
- Organise your notes into sections and chunks.

Structuring

- Develop an essay plan.
- Note the key points for the introduction.
- Interpret the question.

- Note the key points in each part of the essay.
- Which examples will you use to support your points?
- Make sure your conclusion is a firm answer to the question and that it relates to your introduction.

Checking

- Identify the subheadings.
- Make sure all notes fit into a subheading.
- Write out the key points from your essay.
- Put some detail under each key point.
- Check your key points with those in the essay.
- What are the implications from your key points?
- Remember, writing notes is an active way of learning, rather than passive.

Writing

- Write simply and directly.
- Limit your sentence length.
- Ensure that each paragraph has a focus.
- Take care to acknowledge the work of others, and include references.
- Proofread for meaning, then for grammar.
- Ask yourself if the presentation is clear enough.

Write, recite, repeat

"One of the main difficulties experienced by dyslexic students is the use of short- and long-term memory."

Students should have a personal notebook in which they can write down notes and make a daily 'to do' list.

When noting the information in their book, the student could:

- write it down – the actual process of writing can help strengthen the kinaesthetic memory
- recite it to themselves, or to others – this strengthens the memory through both the speech and auditory channels
- repeat it a number of times – this can help them absorb the information through the auditory channel
- annotate the notes with visual symbols and key words – this helps to develop visual skills.

This method is multisensory as it involves the full range of learning skills – seeing, listening, writing, saying and doing. Students can use this 'write, recite, repeat' method for most areas of work involving memory, such as spelling rules, history facts and mathematics problems.

- Look – visual
- Listen – auditory
- Write – kinaesthetic
- Say – verbal
- Do – tactile

Proofreading

"This appears so simple an activity, but I can assure you it is not; it can be very challenging for my students with dyslexia."

Proofreading is an important activity, and the student with dyslexia can find this very challenging.

When we read we usually use context and make a number of inferences. In other words, to read efficiently we do not consciously read every word.

Students with dyslexia tend to focus on the key words or have to read re-read a number of times to get the accuracy and the meaning. This makes proofreading laborious. If they are close to sitting important exams, or if they are doing a project, try pairing them up with another student with dyslexia so they can proofread each other's work.

We usually recommend that students with dyslexia proofread twice: once for meaning, and once for accuracy. For meaning they just do a straightforward read. But for accuracy they should read it sentence by sentence and look for the following:

- obvious spelling mistakes
- sentences that are too long
- not enough paragraphs
- punctuation – capitals especially
- correct word used if there are other, similar words – for example using 'incringe' (note, this is not a real word) when they mean impinge
- correct prepositions used.

Students should make a table in their notebook with the following headings: Title of essay, Spelling, Sentence length, Punctuation, Meaning, Grammar. They can use this as a checklist.

> **Teaching tip**
>
> Proofreading in pairs can be a useful activity, and it is a good idea to pair the student with dyslexia with a student who is not dyslexic. Each will be able to offer their partner some advice. This can be especially good for the student with dyslexia, as they will be able to contribute to their partner's work in some way.

Making connections – think-link-wink

"We should be trying to help students with dyslexia make connections across the curriculum, for effective learning."

Making connections is what learning is all about. It indicates that the student has understood the concept and is able to apply it.

English is a prime subject for this. Words can be introduced that relate to Biology (see Idea 61) and all other subjects, and the connections should be made at the time. This will be helpful for the student.

Effective learning also depends on how readily the learner can make connections between the ideas of the material to be learned with previous learning. The student may ask themselves: How does this relate to what I already know? What else do I need to find out? Have I done this in any other subject?

The aim of this approach is to secure and deepen learning by activating and connecting students' knowledge to other topics and subject areas both in and out of school.

In pairs the students take a paragraph each from their current novel study. They then identify the paragraph they are going to discuss, then show what it means – e.g. is there a deeper meaning, any inferences, or should we take it literally?

Then they link it to some topic/event or idea inside or outside of school. The students then assess it:

- five winks = brilliant
- four winks = very good
- three winks = good
- two winks = not bad
- one wink = keep thinking!

Re-reading for comprehension

"All secondary school teachers must appreciate that students with dyslexia need more time to re-read for comprehension."

Students with dyslexia have often to re-read several times for accuracy and then several times more for comprehension.

Reading for comprehension can be challenging – depending on the level of the passage. Here are some tips that can help.

First, students need to have an adequate **background knowledge** of the text. This helps them place the text in context and develop schema relating to the text.

They also need to ensure that they can understand the **vocabulary** used in the text.

They should take the passage in **small pieces** – paragraph by paragraph or page by page; a chapter may be too long – and then break to ask themselves comprehension questions.

They need to have **questions in mind** as they are reading through the passage – such as 'why', 'what', 'where', 'how' and 'so what'; i.e. the implications – what does it all mean?

At the end of the re-reading sessions they need to be able to **summarise** what they have read in one or two sentences.

Test the student after they have completed the re-reading. They should cover up the passage, then you give them a game called 'four facts and two fibs'. You present a typed sheet of paper, which must include six statements based on the passage – four true and two false (fibs). The false statements need to be believable and not obvious. The student should also write a sentence to explain why they think the fibs are false.

Taking it further

Once students have completed the book and have had opportunities to develop comprehension through re-reading, you can develop a game show based on the book.

- Select a host.
- Choose two 'contestants' who have both read the book.
- Have regular rounds and a bonus round for extra points.
- Make sure the questions relate exactly to the book.
- Make sure the prize is desirable and motivational!

Review notes

"I always give the student time for this – it is so important."

It is best to review notes the same day, as the memory trace can recede very quickly and the information will be lost. If the student waits until the next day or the end of the week, the information may well have little meaning.

Make time each day for reviewing that day's work and any notes that have been made. It is more likely that the dyslexic student will be able to read notes they have written themselves – even if the spelling is wrong – rather than someone else's notes.

They should not attempt to learn too much information in one sitting. The key to minimising loss of information from the memory is to study in short bouts, and frequently. After each short period of study the student should review the notes before moving on to the next piece of information.

To review the notes the student should ask themselves some questions about the notes. Prepare a list of questions for the student to refer to.

- What are the notes about?
- What new information do they provide?
- What strategies should I use to remember the information?
- How can I reorganise them to make them more valuable to me?
- Do they have headings and subheadings?
- How will I separate the information if I colour-code the page?

Finally, the student should be able to write a summary of the notes. It is best to do this every few pages or less.

Print size/page layout/font

"Presentation is so important, and this can make all the difference for students with dyslexia. If the print is too small they will not read it and will pass it by."

The importance of print size and the actual style of the print cannot be overestimated. There are so many possible variations, so it is worthwhile spending some time selecting those that are best suited to the learner with dyslexia.

The page of a worksheet should be organised in a visually appealing manner, and it is important to use a 'dyslexia-friendly' font.

Comic Sans, Century Gothic and Times New Roman are all considered dyslexia-friendly fonts. Establish the student's preferences – for example:

- Do you prefer to read in this font? (Times New Roman)
- Do you prefer to read in this one? (Comic Sans)
- Or do you prefer to read in this style? (Century Gothic)

When you are considering the page layout:

- do not crowd the page
- use larger type
- use visuals where necessary
- remember to space out the information, using the whole page if appropriate
- use indents for headings, subheadings and main text
- use a bold font to highlight headings and/or key points
- fold the paper so you create a fold line for the student to come back to.

Bonus Idea ★

Time to change!

You can make this into a game – take the same piece of text and format it into different font styles (at least six) and presentation. Make a league table of all the timings and the key feature. This can be a fun activity so it is a good idea to do this in pairs and you can also see how you partner performed and note if he/she was different from you. Remember to note that font that is best for you!

Taking it further

The student can also practise using different font styles by themselves when they are working on the laptop. Encourage them to try a few different fonts and then say which one they prefer, and why.

History

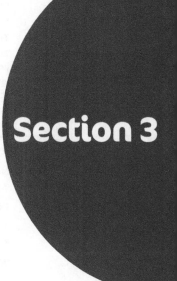

Section 3

Make a timeline

"Everybody needs a timeline, but for history it is essential – the students like doing this, too."

Making a timeline helps the student with dyslexia with organisation and sequencing, and gives them the opportunity to develop each of the events on the timeline. It can also be developed using multimedia sources, and can be made very user friendly.

There are a number of ways of developing a timeline, from making a straightforward list in a linear fashion to more elaborate methods using visuals and PowerPoint. Whatever method the student chooses, it is best to provide them with a structure to ensure the timeline covers all the events correctly. It is a good idea to start by selecting topics and making timelines on these, so there are mini timelines and then a master one.

Note the important events in the topic, e.g. History in the Middle Ages:

Politics and religion

- Governments and rulers
- The role of religion and changes

Warfare

- The most important battles – crusades
- Famous warriors

Trade and commerce

- Agriculture and equipment
- Trade – who sells what to whom

People to remember

- Famous names
- Friends and villains

Provide a framework for your timeline. It is a good idea to make a linear one first, and then elaborate from there.

Who is who – keeping a record of the characters

"Remembering that different characters can be confusing for students with dyslexia – especially remembering the popes and the monarchs, and their numbers or names."

Knowing the characters is like knowing the ingredients for a meal you are about to make. You need to know all the parts and what they do, and how they contribute to the finished product.

Students with dyslexia can easily get the characters in history confused – especially the kings and queens, with all the Henrys, Jameses and Charleses. The difficulty is in remembering all the names, what they did and when. This is **not** what History is about, but the basic ingredients have got to be known before the student can start on the interesting part – so we have to think of painless ways of ensuring they know who is who.

Drama and kinesthetic activities are the best way to do this: not just reading about what the character said, but actually saying it! Get the student to copy out a few famous or important phrases said by the character. They may get this from the Internet, book or play (even one about the character).

Get the students to work in pairs for this; they each have to say a sentence that the famous person said (or may have said). There is a lot of good learning taking place here, as the student may need to read between the lines in order to extract meaning.

They can then write out the comments in a chart and next to each write the period of history and the importance of that comment. They will remember this more effectively, though, if they have actually said the phrase meaningfully to another person.

Taking it further

This activity lends itself to drama and plays. The students can make up their own play on the characters using the phrases. This can be made into a game in which the other students have to guess the character.

Remembering information

"People remember poems and ditties, and it is good fun to pun."

History is not about memory — we must be clear on that. But the student does need to know a certain amount of information, and know why it is important.

This is a challenge for students with dyslexia, and it can also be a challenge for the teacher! It is important to present the information in an active manner and allow the student to develop the information in a creative and personal way. One idea is to make stories, poems or even puns about an event or character – without in any way belittling the importance of the event.

For example:

'Henry the Eighth had five wives and a headmistress!'

'Churchill is that dog that can't sing and sells insurance on the telly!'
(by Donall Dempsey)

Make a list of key people and events in the topic you are studying in History and say why these are important. Then you can try to make up a poem about it – the funnier the better.

This type of activity can be done in pairs but it might also be a good idea if everyone in the class contributed each with one line and a group of people had to put all the lines in some sort of order – and they can also try to make it funny too.

Finding out – investigation

"A good learner is one who knows the questions to ask. Learners with dyslexia can often ask the right questions, and sometimes quite unusual questions. It is important to encourage this."

This is really what History is all about — not memory and regurgitating facts, but investigating and finding out.

There are many different ways of doing this, and some of these are shown in this primer idea for investigation.

Technology – This holds the key; investigation using the Internet can make history come to life. Pre-investigating discussion is important to make sure students know the right questions to ask. Once they have a bank of questions or points, they can put these into the search engine. However, it is important that they do not waste time and digress to less important aspects of the topic.

What, why and so what?

You could divide the questions into **core questions** (the what; essential for background and events), **important questions** (the why; lets you know why something happened and gives you an idea of the context and the events leading up to the topic under investigation), and **'so what' questions** – these look at the implications stemming from the event or topic.

The student can divide their page into three columns using these headings.

Taking it further

You can use this idea for other topics such as current issues in society – values, social issues and topics relating to the students' own lifestyles. It is a good idea to practise with those types of issues, as they are relatively content free. It is important to reinforce the point that there is not necessarily a right or wrong answer to the task, as long as students can justify their response.

Field trips

"It is important to take advantage of field trips – they are an essential part of learning, and of course fun for the student."

Field trips have the potential to be extremely beneficial for students with dyslexia. They can help them understand concepts and provide a visual experience of the topic they are studying. Field trips also encourage experiential learning which promotes a deeper learning experience.

Fieldwork can also be used to develop skills in research as well as data collection, and the use of specialist equipment in some subjects. Additionally it can develop students' observational abilities in the landscape and environmental interpretations, as in the example below on a battlefield.

It is important that the experience and the activities to be carried out are presented in a structured and accessible manner. It is important therefore to prepare the students for the trip. This would include the where, the why and the purpose of the trip. It is important to provide the students with a set of objectives at the outset that should be achieved during the trip. The activity below highlights a possible checklist to ensure the student keeps on track during the trip and that the purpose of the trip is achieved. This type of activity can also be carried out in pairs.

Planning

You are visiting a famous battlefield – there are many that spring to mind, such as Bannockburn and Culloden in Scotland, Evesham and Hastings in England or St Fagan's in Wales.

Pre-field trip

It is important that the students have background knowledge of the battle – this would include the armies and their size, how they were equipped and the time of day as well as the month of the year. They need to know what the weather would have been like at the time. The battle and the outcome are equally important.

Field trip checklist

- Identify the key positions in the battlefield – take a photo of the positions where the armies would have stood at the beginning of the battle.
- Identify other aspects of position such as hills, valleys, river and closeness to towns for supplies.
- Take a photo of where the main part of the battle was fought.
- Obtain information from the visitor centre or the Internet on the battle, and write a paragraph on how it developed and the outcome.
- Can you now try to give some reasons why it ended like it did?

Here you might give them a list of seven or eight different reasons, and they have to rank them. This would be particularly helpful for students with dyslexia.

In conclusion, students can comment on what they learned during the trip. Encourage them to restrict this to one sentence.

What to look out for

It is important not to assume that all students will find fieldwork easy and accessible. There are many factors in fieldwork that can present a challenge for students with dyslexia. For example, they can have problems taking notes, writing at speed, organising the time they have to spend there, with directional orientation and perhaps map reading, and with remembering the actual arrangements for the field trip and the design of the written materials (they need to be visual and colourful, with adequate space).

See it, feel it, do it – acting the part

"Multisensory learning is the key – experience and activity are essential for effective learning."

History lends itself to experiential learning – all new learning in a history topic can be acted out.

Students with dyslexia will not absorb the information if it is only geared to the listening modality. It is a good idea to start with the minimum of listening, quickly added to by activities and drama. Try to encourage first-person dialogue, as this will also help to develop some reality in the topic under discussion. Ensure that visuals have been used (see it), that experiential learning is involved and that there is ample scope for activities.

This type of activity can be carried out in groups. This can also take away some of the embarrassment that students may feel when acting out a particular scene in history.

Provide a structure for the students and give them a specific task to act out. For example, if they are studying the Industrial Revolution in Britain, this could involve the factory owner speaking to their workers about the rules of working, then the workers discussing these. This way both sides of the situation can be seen – the employer's and the worker's. This can lend itself to a debate on working and living conditions. It can also help the student get involved in the situation and help to bring some understanding of different perspectives.

Provide pictures of the characters involved and allocate each of these to the students. They can then be sure of what the character they are portraying actually stands for, and other details about them and their family.

Geography

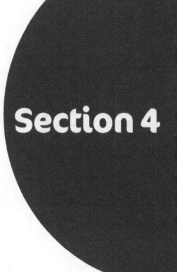

Section 4

Understanding maps

"Maps can be simplified and made more readable — so let's make maps dyslexia friendly."

Map reading involves a lot of different skills — visual/spatial and directional skills, understanding shapes and contours, compass skills and, very importantly, a new language — technical terms will also need to be explained.

Taking it further

You can make a glossary of terms that are usually used in map reading, and the glossary can be complemented by a visual. This can include words such as contour, gradient, latitude, chart, nautical, coordinates, elevation, estuary, grid, hydrography, landmark, longitude, meridian, aerial, orientation, projection, quadrangle, relief, topography, tide, zenith telescope.

One of the most complex maps in existence must be the London Underground map. Many attempts have been made to simplify it, but it is still the most difficult of maps to follow. With only a little imagination and dyslexia-friendly ideas, much can be done to improve this for people with dyslexia.

Similarly with conventional maps — they can be confusing and unclear with small print, and a number of assumptions about map reading can be inferred. Below are some ideas to consider when developing maps for students with dyslexia. People with dyslexia are very visual, so it is a good idea to use as many visual landmarks as possible in a map.

- Take any map at all that you want to make dyslexia friendly.
- Write down the key landmarks — e.g. hills, major roads, buildings of interest, rivers, and the starting point — where you are at the moment.
- Obtain visuals, in the form of small photos, of these landmarks.
- Put them on the map in the appropriate place.
- Mark the suggested route you want to take in a bright colour.
- Photocopy the map at two sizes — one very large and one pocket size.
- Prepare the student for the map-reading exercise by using the visual landmarks to complete a mind map.

Time zones and climates

"Understanding time zones and different climates is a lifelong skill and one that is very useful."

Though this is an extremely useful skill, it is one that students with dyslexia can find baffling and confusing.

Time zones can be a difficult concept to understand, and it needs to be explained to students. They need to appreciate the big picture regarding the relationship between the Sun and the Earth – this concept must be fully explained before advancing to discussion of specific time zones.

The following activity can be a popular one with students, as it involves a mobile phone or their laptop. The world clock icon on mobile phones or computer apps is an analogue clock for each country, and it is usually black at night, and white in the daytime.

Students should select one or two countries in each continent, then choose a city and look up the time in that city and store it in their phone. They can then refer to it when necessary.

They can also transfer this to a drawing in their notebooks – they should select a time, e.g. 12 noon in the UK or their home country, and work out the time in other countries when it is 12 noon in the UK (or their country). They can then draw all the clocks showing the various times, and keep it to refer to.

Taking it further

Students can look at international flight timetables and note the departure and arrival times of some flights going in both directions – eastwards and westwards – and note the comparisons.

Making charts and graphs

"Charts and graphs are really another language for some dyslexic students."

Students with dyslexia can be quite inventive and creative visually, if they are given a free hand. But charts and graphs are more restrictive and logical, and often require sequential and analytical thinking.

Taking it further

This task can be done in pairs, and students may put it into a PowerPoint presentation and customise an animation so that each section or colour on the chart is added separately. This can make it much clearer for the student with dyslexia.

Students with dyslexia are more inclined to be random and holistic thinkers; charts and graphs and other similar visual statistics can be challenging for them to interpret. These therefore have to be made dyslexia friendly.

The use of colour is important to differentiate between the different parts of the graph or chart. Every chart can have a colour key, and the same with the graphs. It is a good idea to get students to make their own key and their own chart based on something that is familiar to them. For example, how they spend their pocket money or the results of the football game highlighting the highest/lowest scorers.

Data – Columns – Colour – Text

This formula can help the student remember what has to be done and the order of doing it.

The **data** is the information they need to put into the graph or chart. This needs to be gathered beforehand and discussed with you or a peer. It is important that the correct data is identified.

The **columns** can follow after that – the student should decide whether it should be a graph or chart, or any other type of diagram.

Colour is important. Colours should be selected to stand out from each other.

The **text** can help the student interpret the graph or chart – e.g., an explanation or glossary.

Using technical words

"Having a knowledge and understanding of the relevant technical and specialised words is essential before the student starts to learn about a topic in any detail."

Every subject will have some specialised words. It is important to introduce the student with dyslexia to those words at an early stage so they have a sound understanding of what they refer to.

In geography there will be quite a number of specialised words due to the nature of the subject. Don't take it for granted that the dyslexic student will know even common words – they may not, or they may misinterpret the meaning of a word.

Providing the key words and allowing the student to absorb these into their schema for each subject is important.

Make a visual representation of the key words and what they mean. Provide a sentence and leave space for the student to do this too.

You can provide some of the words – the most common ones – and get the student to look up some other possible key words the Internet or discuss them with others in the class.

The student should allocate a notebook to key words. For example, Idea 34 suggests a glossary of key words and gives examples such as contour, gradient, latitude, chart, nautical, coordinates, elevation, estuary, grid, hydrography, landmark, longitude, meridian, aerial, orientation, projection, quadrangle, relief, topography, tide and zenith telescope. The student can print out (from the Internet) an image to represent each of these key words, or draw them themselves.

This notebook can become each student's own reference book.

Taking it further

This activity can be completed for all subjects – some examples of vocabulary are shown in Idea 17.

Making Geography real

"This is a subject that can easily become very dyslexia friendly, as it can involve lots of investigation and discovery."

Students with dyslexia need multisensory teaching and learning — with active and experiential learning. Geography is one of the subjects that lends itself best to this type of learning.

Develop a checklist or table that can help you to monitor the use of multisensory strategies in each of the topics you teach in Geography. This is also revision of the ideas highlighted in this section on Geography.

Two examples are shown below :

1. Topic – Map reading

Aim – Understand the different aspects of map reading.

Mutisensory strategies – Make own map – cut and paste – discussion with others in group.

Materials used – Scissors, maps, paper, coloured crayons.

2. Topic – Climate change

Aim – Understand reasons for climate change and its impact on civilisations.

Mutisensory strategies – YouTube video on climate change, examples from different continents at different times of year.

Materials used – Videos, interviews with local people on climate change in their own country, look up people on the Internet people who have experienced severe climate change.

Mathematics

Section 5

The language of Maths

"The terminology and language of Maths can be significant barriers for dyslexic students."

It is important that the meanings of terminology and technical words are made clear.

Teaching tip

Get the student themselves to make an icon for each of these words or terms. You can give an example, but students will become more familiar with the terms if they use their own icons.

Anne Henderson, a Maths and dyslexia expert, indicates that 'Maths is a foreign language so we need to translate from Maths to English and English to Maths. Mathematics is a second language and should be taught as such. It is exclusively bound to the symbolic representation of ideas. Most of the difficulties seen in mathematics result from the underdevelopment of the language of mathematics.' (Henderson, 2003)

Be proactive and identify words that may be challenging for the dyslexic student. It is useful to provide a visual to represent each, along with an explanation and an example.

Words/terms that can be challenging:

- Sequencing
- Fractions
- Decimal place
- Estimate
- Position, e.g. under, over, beside, next to, outside, inside, in front, behind, beside, on top, at the bottom, forwards, backwards, sideways, turn
- Quantities, e.g. many, few, more, less, same as
- Measures, e.g. long, short, heavy, light, full, empty
- Shapes, e.g. circle, square, triangle, rectangle, star, pentagon, octagon, ball, cube
- Two-dimensional and three-dimensional
- Calculations, e.g. add, sum of, plus, total, subtract, minus, take away, double, left over, difference

Taking it further

You can help to develop and extend students' conceptual understanding of some of these terms at the same time as they are developing the glossary.

Making Maths simple

"It is crucial that students with dyslexia are active learners in Maths, and that the steps used are simple and clear."

Maths needs to be simplified for many students with dyslexia. Terminology, concepts, presentation and assessment are all challenging.

It is interesting to reflect on the points made by Askew (2013) on Maths teaching, which indicated that the better qualified in mathematics teachers were, the lower the average class gains. Additionally the research showed that there was a positive association between class gains and the amount of in-service training undertaken, and that the length of service in the teaching profession did not indicate effective teaching. The research also asked students what aspects of Maths teaching they found challenging. The responses included: 'not telling us clearly enough what to do', 'copying all the time from the board', 'teacher having bad handwriting', 'telling us, not showing us' and 'too much writing'. The points below indicate how to overcome these challenges when teaching Maths.

- Lots of oral and practical work.
- Discussion and videos about a new Maths topic.
- Slow down and repeat.
- Larger desks so students can build shapes and work in a practical way.
- More wall displays.
- More active learning and group discussion.
- Recognise different learning styles.
- More use of colour, highlighter pens, counting equipment, Dienes blocks, partition cards, number sticks, number fans, individual whiteboards and pens.
- Start each lesson with a recap of the previous one and ensure it has been fully understood.

Taking it further

Dyslexic students can experience the following difficulties with Maths:

- remembering rules and formulae
- sequencing the order and value of numbers
- tracking up and down the number line
- learning basic symbols
- estimating and checking their answers
- learning times tables
- rounding up and down with regard to place value
- properties of shapes; unable to connect the formula to the correct shape or process.

Presenting Maths work

"How information is presented is very important – it can mean the difference between 'Yes I can do this' or 'No I can't'!"

This can apply to all subjects, but it is particularly important in Maths that the page or worksheet is presented in a way that can be easily accessed by the student with dyslexia.

One of the key considerations is space – in other words, do not crowd the page. The dyslexic student is inclined to miss lines if they are too close together.

- Limit lines to 60 characters of text.
- Leave ample space between examples.
- Use headings for each example.
- Use short sentences.
- Use bold or colour to highlight – do not use italics or underline, as this can make words run together.
- Align text left; don't justify.
- Use bullet points or numbers rather than continuous text.
- Don't split words between lines by hyphenating.
- The space between lines is important – the suggested amount is 1.5 to 2 times a space.
- Have the main instructions within text boxes.
- Centre text boxes on the page.
- Don't make box outlines too thick.
- Use an accessible typeface – Ariel is good. There are other good ones, and it might be an idea to work this out with the student.
- Use lower case rather than capitals where possible.

Taking it further

Here are some more points to consider when making worksheets.

- Don't make the worksheet over-stimulating to the eye.
- Have a contents page explaining what the worksheet is about and how long it should take .
- Use a repeating icon at the top of each page to link the sheets together. Make it appropriate.
- Colour-coding can help the student group the different tasks.
- Use cream or off-white paper. Don't use glossy paper.

Technology and Maths

"Thank goodness for technology – at last Maths can be fun!"

There is no doubt at all that technology has been a huge boost for students with dyslexia.

It can simplify concepts, help the student engage in active learning...and above all, it can be fun.

There are many computer games and programs available – the problem arises when selecting those that are appropriate for the secondary school student with dyslexia. Some of the programs for dyscalculia will be of benefit for the dyslexic student – it is a good idea to try a demonstration first. You may also go for one that looks easier and below the age level of the student. This will increase their confidence and motivation.

The programme **Maths Explained** includes videos by Steve Chinn (an internationally recognised Maths specialist) – his work and the videos are underpinned by Steve's research and experience, and on research from leading experts from around the world. This program illustrates concepts simply and unlocks learning barriers. The lessons also provide a solid foundation, and the students work at their own pace.

http://www.stevechinn.co.uk/about.html
www.mathsexplained.co.uk

Fluid Math is award-winning educational software that enables teachers and students to create, solve, graph and animate Maths (and Physics) problems all in their own handwriting on the screen of a tablet PC or interactive whiteboard. For teachers, it is designed to assist in creating instructional materials to provide engaging learning experiences. For students, it is designed to help explore and understand concepts in mathematics and science.

http://www.fluiditysoftware.com

Teaching tip

Computer games provide excellent learning experiences and can help with processing speed and reaction times. They can also help with attention and concentration – it is important to pass this message across to parents but it is also crucial that the student uses the games appropriately.

Bonus Idea

Slot Car Challenge

Designed for years 8-10 this is challenging and competitive.

The player must finish three laps within a set time to unlock further vehicles and tracks. The student can keep a record of their performances, complete practice laps and analyse these on their laptop.

http://splash.abc.net.au/slotcars-game/game

Memory and Maths

"We all know that students with dyslexia can have difficulties with memory, so we should try to minimise the memory load."

Memory – both working memory and long-term memory – can be problematic for students with dyslexia. It is important to try to minimise the impact of this.

Taking it further

Encourage the students to make up their own mnemonics – that way they will be more likely to remember them, and use them.

They might do this for:

- Months of the Year
- Seasons
- Properties of squares, triangles and rectangles
- Different types of triangles, e.g. scalene, isosceles
- Different types of angles, e.g. acute, obtuse

Students can make drawings of these and add in some explanation. They could also make a poem or song out of them.

There are various memory tricks and mnemonics that can be used to help students remember some basic Maths rules. It is worthwhile spending a little time to help them use these strategies.

For example, posters displaying information on basic Maths signs such as 'multiply, 'add', 'equals' and so on, can provide a visual reminder of what each of these signs mean. Although it is likely that the student will know these signs they may still need reminders – particularly if they are working at speed and stressed. Try to provide clear visual prompts that require a minimum of reading. It is also important to remember that dyslexic students can usually only cope with one or two steps at a time. Avoid including too many steps in problems, as this will overload the memory.

- Develop a sequence checklist – this will be a checklist for different calculations, which will also indicate which rules to use.
- Make a personal checklist for the student, and use colour-coding and visual images on personal timetables. This acts as a reminder of what has to be done, and when.
- Use rhymes to remember information:
  - *Try to remember the following thought*
  - *Even numbers end 2, 4, 6, 8 or nought.*
  - *Remember, remember the following rhyme*
  - *Odd numbers end 1, 3, 5, 7 or nine.*

Maths learning styles

"It is important to consider the student's learning style, as this can make all the difference to them understanding a problem."

Learning styles or learning preferences is an important factor that can enhance learning, and this is certainly the case in Maths.

Dr Steve Chinn is credited with devising and popularising the learning styles framework shown below – **Inchworms and Grasshoppers**. Ask students how they feel about using the different types of apparatus and about using their own learning preference in Maths.

Inchworm characteristics	Grasshopper Characteristics
Prescriptive nature	Intuitive nature
Analyses	Holistic
Finds formula	Forms concepts
Looks at facts	Estimates
Has recipe for solution	Uses controlled exploration
Adds straight down	Reverses and adjusts
Writes down	Solves inside head
Tends to do + and −	Tends to do x and ÷

Preferred Apparatus

Inchworm	Grasshopper
Number lines	Dienes blocks
Multilink	cuisinaire rods
Counting blocks	Graph paper and grids
Unifix cubes	geoboards
Paper and pencil	Attribute blocks

(Adapted from learning-works.org.uk)

Taking it further

You can look at other learning styles instruments (see Idea 88) and particularly the those influencing the affective dimension, which looks at persistence, perseverance, frustration and tolerance levels, curiosity, level of independent learning, motivation, risk taking, cautiousness, how they react to competition, eagerness to cooperate with others, reaction to reinforcement and personal interests.

Problems and strategies

"I like the idea of a chart, as I can see at a glance what to do with different problems and issues in Maths."

There can be a range of difficulties experienced by dyslexic learners in Maths.

Taking it further

This type of activity can lend itself to discussion, particularly among senior students. They can discuss the problems they experience in Math and how they have tackled these. Often this exchange of ideas can be very helpful and motivating for students with dyslexia.

This activity suggests using a chart with columns such as 'What to look for' and 'How to help'. Using this technique, you can see at a glance what you need to do to support the student. This can also be a good departmental resource, and can be made into a poster.

Make a chart with two columns: 'What to look for' and 'How to help'.

You can then add to it as you come across problems encountered and new ideas to deal with these problems.

Some examples are shown below:

What to look for – Reading the question accurately.

How to help – Ensure the vocabulary level is right.

What to look for – May rush the work due to speed difficulties.

How to help – Check student's understanding early on, and check this with the student at each step in the method. Consider providing the answer so that students can see where they are heading and know when they have arrived.

What to look for – Not finishing in time.

How to help – Practise timing against the clock, but make it a fun exercise. It may be necessary to offer the student some clues at the beginning so they get off to a good start. See Learning Works for more information on Maths strategies: learning-works.org.uk.

Music, Drama and Art

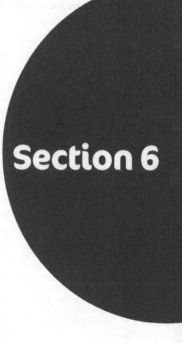

Section 6

Using colour to read music

"We discovered he was watching his piano teacher play a tune, and because he has a strong visual memory he was memorising what his teacher was doing with her hands."

This in turn means that the use of colour to highlight the visual stimulus can be extremely helpful for students with dyslexia.

Not only do they respond better to colour images, but when they are reading music while playing it helps the different notes stand out more clearly. They are often very visual and can learn by watching rather than reading or listening.

Prof. Margaret Hubicki produced the Colour-Staff approach when she was teaching at the Royal Academy of Music in the UK. By using the concept of the circle of fifths in conjunction with the rhyme to accompany the colours of the rainbow – 'Richard Of York Gave Battle In Vain' – she helped students with a combination of rhyme and colour.

The publication *Smarties for Brass* by Robert Miller also uses this approach. It involves a book of scales and arpeggios for trumpet, B^b cornet and flugelhorn based around the ABRSM syllabuses for Grades 1–8. Each of the seven possible valve combination is given a colour, and all scales, arpeggios and exercises are printed with the note heads in the relevant colour and coloured blobs underneath (see www.smartiesforbrass.com).

Do consider whether visual difficulties, such as visual stress, are a problem. If so, try copying the music on tinted paper of the student's choice. The use of colour should also help to alleviate visual stress.

The Top Ten

"The way we teach music traditionally is not that helpful for dyslexics."

It is important to break the traditional mould for teaching music and to highlight a more flexible and individualised approach required by many students with dyslexia.

The opening quote came from Alie Reid, Scottish singer and Churchill Memorial Travel Fellowship award winner.

It is important to ensure that the teaching is right and that there is a degree of awareness among those who teach music that students with dyslexia can have these problems.

The Top Ten

- Recognise and embrace the differences - it is important to be flexible.
- Don't impose ideas on the student.
- Use colour of the student's choice for highlighting the notes and other aspects of the music score.
- The task should be structured, otherwise they may not complete it.
- Use multisensory approaches: hear, see, feel, read, write, and use hands-on activities.
- Consider the potential for visual stress; it is worthwhile using tinted/coloured paper of the student's choice.
- Use overlearning/revision/embedding. Dyslexic students will require a lot of repetition.
- Recognise that dyslexic students usually have short-term/working-memory difficulties. Use summaries so they can recap more easily.
- Presentation and assessment – ensure that the task is presented to the student in a dyslexia-friendly way. Use an appropriate font, space out the work and allow ample time.

Teaching tip

Consider self-esteem

Success is the key and it is important not to let students with dyslexia become intimidated by others who can read music easily and quickly.

Music can be a very competitive pursuit, and it is important to try to minimise the impact of this. Try to look for avenues of positive feedback and to help them feel successful. When giving feedback always start with a positive comment!

Auditory processing and rhythm games

"It is increasingly recognised that engagement with music can support the acquisition of language skills."

It is also recognised that students with dyslexia can have difficulties with auditory processing.

Teaching tip

Some tips for enhancing auditory processing:

- Avoid too much environmental distraction.
- Keep instructions to a minimum.
- Provide reassurance on tasks.
- Split tasks into shorter tasks with frequent breaks.
- Scaffold work.
- Use visual cues and modelling before a task is attempted.
- Use technology.

Taking it further

You must try karaoke – it is ideal for students with dyslexia, as they can hear the beat and the music and read the words at the same time. It is a good idea to practise the words beforehand, in a group to begin with, then in pairs and eventually on their own. They should practise the words a number of times before they try in with the karaoke machine.

The opening quote came from Katie Overy in the book *Music and Dyslexia: A Positive Approach* (Wiley, 2008).

There can in fact be an overlap between auditory processing difficulties (APD) and dyslexia. This means that students with dyslexia are likely to have difficulties listening and processing verbal instructions. It also means that they may have difficulty with discriminating between different sounds and rhythms. It can also mean that the words to a song have to be presented separately, and they should read the lyrics – perhaps in a group or using the paired reading approach – before trying to sing the words to music.

Aural tests, particularly those involving memory, can also be difficult. It is important that accommodations are made for the dyslexic student in relation to this. They will need the sound repeated and more time to complete the exercise. Ideally they should not be tested in this way, and rather judged for their overall performance and creativity.

However, according to the music researcher Katie Overy, the relationship between music and reading can be reciprocal. Materials on developing rhythm and using rhyme and rhythm when reading can help both in music and in reading.

Music, dyslexia and creativity

"A sheet of musical notes just looks like random sticks and balls to me."

Marc Jordan's story is an inspiring one, as he had a long struggle before he realised he was dyslexic.

The opening quote is from Marc Jordan, songwriter (including hits for Diana Ross, Chicago, Bette Midler, Cher, Joe Cocker and Rod Stewart).

It is helpful to listen to the stories of dyslexic people who have been successful in the arts. Many have had struggles that we can learn from.

Marc Jordan had to keep developing strategies such as memorising his piano teachers' movements in order to recreate the music without being able to read the notes on the page. He maintains that when he writes a song, he sees a movie in his head, and adds that he has a knack for making up little stories about anything he sees. His hit 'Living in Marina del Rey' came from a street sign he saw when he was in a taxi coming from the airport to his hotel in Los Angeles. He didn't go there; he just imagined the place.

His wife provided the impetus for him to understand his dyslexia (although he had no name for it at the time). She learned to give him information in small chunks, and check and double-check schedules and dates. He says that the social isolation of his high school years took a huge emotional toll. He chose to speak about his dyslexia because he knows that many students are going through the same thing. (Adapted from source: *Toronto Star*, 8 March 2015).

Taking it further

Create, mix and produce your own songs using GarageBand's built-in instruments.

iPad Music Accessories: http://www.ikmultimedia.com/

Drama – a subject for all seasons

"Overcoming the obstacles of dyslexia came down to simple 'hard graft', and I still have days where reading just won't work."

'Drama is an extremely important subject, and one where the student with dyslexia can excel'. Keira Knightly

Taking it further

Drama can be one of the best of the cross-curricular activities. It can involve the production of stage sets, the design of costumes or the making of masks and puppets, the use of stage lighting and sound effects, and the discovery of suitable props. All of these activities stem directly from the script and involve the students in creative thought and activity, as well as skills used in other subjects.

Drama can also involve the students in discussion about what is required, and makes use of any talents the students may possess. It is therefore possible for other subject teachers to get involved in this and to utilise collaborative partnerships across the curriculum.

The opening quote is from Keira Knightly (BDA Music Committee Newsletter No. 5, February 2014).

Drama lends itself to active participation and kinaesthetic and experiential learning and it is important to make it accessible for students with dyslexia.

There are many activities involving role play that can help with drama, such as the one below.

Role Play and the Freeze Frame

In groups of four, students should talk about a memorable event that happened during the holidays. If nothing interesting happened to them, they must invent something! Then they decide on a freeze frame to start the drama. (A freeze frame is when the students capture a caption and hold it.)

They then bring the drama to life for 30 seconds, and then do it again, but this time using words. They can practise this several times. The events students choose can be quite ordinary, e.g. shopping with friends, or very unusual, e.g. witnessing an accident.

After two minutes stop the class and tell them that they have one minute left to work on their best moment in the drama. During this time you must move about the class helping, questioning and encouraging the students.

Your job is to motivate at this stage. Keeping the students under the pressure of time helps to clarify and focus the role play, otherwise it can ramble.

Now you are ready to bring the freeze frames to life. Get the students to relax, and ask for volunteers to show their freeze frames and role play to the class. Ask each group to hold their freeze frame, and count down '3 – 2 – 1 – GO!' After about 30 seconds say 'And freeze.'

Respect for the students' peers is essential here. Take a bit of time with this. It is important to remind the students that they are practising their audience skills as well as their performance skills.

Extending the role play – a structured activity

You can introduce a structured activity and give the students tasks, such as in the example below.

Select groups of four students. One of the group works for a local paper or TV company, in a seaside town that is very short of news at the moment. One person has to go on to the beach and interview tourists. The rest of the group are the tourists. All of you need to spend one or two minutes deciding what makes a newsworthy item. Practise this for five minutes and then decide how to start with a freeze frame, and be ready to bring it to life for 30 seconds. Set this up as above.

It is important to watch all the groups and to praise them as much as you can.

You are looking for examples of realism, controversy, humour and inventive treatment of the situation. Ideally this should be a very appropriate activity for the dyslexic student, and one which can provide additional benefits in terms of learning and in building their confidence.

Bonus Idea ★

Be a director

A director must have a sound knowledge of the whole process and know what is possible and what is not. It involves many skills such as knowledge of the script, location, actors and acting. It will be good practice to get the students in pairs so the student with dyslexia will not be alone in this and they can be joint directors. Give them a film title and get them to work out how they would direct the film.

Art – investigate, study, explore and invent

"Art and Design is very inclusive as it represents freedom of expression, and all students can do this."

Art is one of the subjects that everyone should be able to do in some way. It can be an important subject for dyslexic students, as it can help them to express themselves in their own way.

Teaching Tip

Art can build a student's self-esteem. It should also help the student become aware of their feelings, imagination and emotions, and help them develop their ideas into a practical product. You can get the students to identify different emotions people experience and then match these to pieces of art.

Art offers a great choice of activities; it is inherently a multisensory subject and therefore is well suited to the dyslexic student. It is a fact that there is a high percentage of dyslexic students at art colleges throughout the UK.

Certainly being dyslexic should not prevent someone from excelling at Art. In fact the current view is that those with dyslexia can often solve problems and develop products in a way that may be out of reach for others who think more linearly.

It is interesting to reflect on the words of Tom West (West 1997), who indicated that 'people with dyslexia can see the unseen'. This means that they can be inventive, and will often see a new or different angle to a problem.

Activities

Get the students to do or make something that will benefit the community. For example:

- designing squares for a 'special occasion' quilt
- making puppets for a school or community play
- experimenting with shapes and patterns for decorations for school events
- designing their own memory game or game that can develop processing speed
- decorating clocks depicting time zones in different countries – this links with Geography
- Using papier mâché to show land formations, which can also link with Geography.

General Science

Section 7

Labelling the laboratory

"Students with dyslexia can often excel in Science subjects because there is less need for extended writing and they are able to focus on content."

A detailed and labelled plan of the science laboratory is essential for dyslexic students.

Teaching tip

You can ask the students to work out – perhaps in pairs – why the laboratory is laid out the way it is. This can lead on to logical thinking and safety considerations. The idea is to get the student with dyslexia to work this out for themselves.

Students with dyslexia need a structure to give them a clear understanding of what to do in a task. They also need to be familiar with the routines of the classroom, as well as where resources and apparatus is kept. The science laboratory must be well organised, for safety reasons. You could present the students with a plan of the laboratory, but it will have more impact if students with dyslexia do this for themselves.

Step 1 – Make a list of all the apparatus and locations in the laboratory.

Step 2 – Draw the outline of the laboratory and indicate where the key points are – e.g. door, windows, cupboards, teacher's desk, your own desk, and wall displays and other fixed items.

Step 3 – Transfer this to your laptop.

Step 4 – Make an icon for all the apparatus that you have listed in Step 1. This can be any type of icon – then you can make a glossary, with the word matching the icon.

Step 5 – Draw the icon on the appropriate page on your paper, and also on your laptop version.

Step 6 – Check your finished version with a partner.

Step 7 – If you are happy with it, stick the paper version inside the back cover of your Science notebook. Save the computer version in your Science folder on your laptop.

Conducting experiments

"Students with dyslexia need clear, logical, short, achievable targets in science."

The student with dyslexia can display many strengths that will be of particular use in Science.

- Lateral thinking – a different approach to problem solving.
- Ability to design more interesting and perhaps unorthodox experiments.
- Contributing to innovative ideas.
- Asking insightful questions.
- Working well in teams or with one other person.

It is important that they are able to use these skills, which will only be possible if the task or the activity is structured for them. This section on Science will highlight these supports.

Taking it further

You can ask the student to note all the science words used in the experiment and to add these to the glossary they are compiling. It might also be a good idea to add an icon for all the words in the glossary.

- Pair the dyslexic student with a good reader. There may not be many instructions, but it is crucial that they are read accurately.
- Explain that diagrams that may appear in the text, and show how they can replace the written text. A good diagram should reduce text to a minimum.
- Provide a full explanation of the diagram or any graphs that may appear on the text.
- Indicate the laboratory equipment that will be used, and show a picture of it beside the text.
- You may also want to provide a glossary of the terms that are to be used.
- Give the student a demonstration of the experiment that is to be carried out.
- The student can then carry out the experiment but monitor progress as they go.
- The student should then write up a short report on the experiment. Try to encourage the student to add points of reflection. What did the student learn from the exercise?

Reporting on experiments

"Students with dyslexia can have great ideas, but the difficulty they can experience when reporting on an experiment can minimise the impact."

Many famous scientists almost missed out on getting their inventions known because they were not able to record them appropriately. In fact many had to rely on demonstration, and this is one of the strong areas for students with dyslexia.

Teaching tip

Permit to use alternatives to writing when recording results, for example dictation. This is very useful for dyslexic students.

However, the curriculum – and particularly the exam system – means that the experiment has to be written up in an appropriate manner. Students with dyslexia can have poor sequencing skills as well as experiencing organisational difficulties, and this means that reporting can be challenging.

As noted for other subjects, a structure is essential for reporting information. In Science accuracy is crucial in terms of the outcome, process and sequence.

Step 1 – Provide the key points in the experiment and the words you are likely to use.

Step 2 – Students should highlight the apparatus they have used and explain why and how these were accessed (use the glossary if it helps).

Step 3 – Introduce the actual experiment – this is a scene-setting exercise indicating the purpose of the experiment and the context.

Step 4 – Students are to write a paragraph detailing the results – this should be very factual, perhaps using a graph or bullet points.

Step 5 – Students are to write a paragraph commenting on the results.

Step 6 – Note the challenges and obstacles the student had to overcome and to note these for future reference.

Grasping the concept

"Because the student with dyslexia is preoccupied with the facts they often miss out on the vital concepts of the topic."

The above point is very true in science. Dyslexic students may struggle to retain the technical vocabulary, the formulae and the procedures of the experiment.

It is important to ensure that the underlying concept is clear in each activity. Give students the facts – after they have done the experiment and reported on it. This will alleviate the burden of them having to recall what they did. Provide this in the form of a flow chart, as this will help them see the main points in the experiment.

Science concepts can be grasped best through multisensory learning: animations, videos, pictures, computer software and field trips.

In some topics in Science, the task is to put certain events in the correct order.

- In the experiment there may be a list of six or seven key aspects to be labelled from A to F and put in order. Dyslexic students should write down the letters A B C D E F and cross each one off as they use it.
- They should then highlight the key words; after each of the letters they need to show in bold what it means. This can be difficult for them, so they could work with a partner.
- There will usually be some reading associated with this, and it can be difficult for them to process the information; use mind maps, mnemonics and bullet-pointed revision sheets to help.
- Opportunities for group discussion and presentations to the class will enable all students to process the information themselves and achieve a deeper conceptual level of learning.

Teaching tip

There are many opportunities in the laboratory setting to demonstrate initiative and an enquiring mind, and this is to the advantage of dyslexic students.

Get the environment right

"You do not really understand something unless you can explain it to your grandmother." – Albert Einstein

Science is a part of the curriculum where dyslexic students can achieve well, if their needs are met sensitively and appropriately.

Taking it further

Posters for motivation

Although there are some excellent posters available to buy, do get the students to make their own posters, both on safety and on the joys of science. For example, they might call it 'Science is Fun and Safe'. This type of activity is very dyslexia friendly, but it should be carried out in a group.

The environment in the science class should be stimulating in order to prompt investigation and learning through discovery. However, all the dangers in a science laboratory it can be quite frightening. Apparatus can be fragile and it can be quite easy to knock things over, so it is important that the students are aware of this.

This is particularly important for the student with dyslexia, as there can be an overlap between dyslexia and dyspraxia – and even if not, dyslexic students may still have some attention and coordination issues. For this reason it is important that there is consistency and that they know where things are in the lab.

It is also important that the classroom environment offers the opportunity for effective and flexible learning and that the environment is learner friendly, for example, ensuring the student does not have their back to the teacher or the board, as this can make it difficult for a dyslexic student to cope with writing tasks if information is being dictated.

It is important to provide a learning-rich and flexible environment, but that safety guidelines are adhered to. It is useful to reinforce the safety message to dyslexic students, as they can be prone to distraction or lose concentration.

Biology

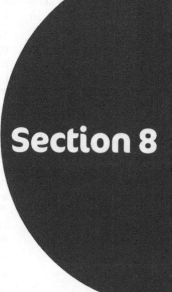

Section 8

Using the 'technical words' in Biology

"Accurate learning and recollection of names is a real problem for the student with dyslexia."

Biology is a subject that contains a vast amount of factual details and many new technical words.

Taking it further

It is important to remember that some words specific to Biology have unfamiliar letter combinations, e.g. *ae*, *ch* = k sound, *psy*. Gradually build up a collection of 'master sheets' which can be photocopied, to enable students to practise these words at home.

These words are rarely used in everyday speech, so they have to be specifically learned for Biology. They are often long words with Latin or Greek-style spellings which may readily be confused when visually similar, e.g. mitosis/meiosis. It is important that these words are not copied from the board, as the dyslexic student is likely to make errors.

Many of the words are quite technical and specialised, usually quite abstract and certainly not everyday words, e.g. homeostasis, ecosystem and mesosystem. The spelling of these words is also very important, as there can be very slight and subtle differences in the spellings.

There are two aspects to remembering and using the specialised words. One is the understanding, i.e. what the word means and what it refers to. The other is the accurate spelling of the word.

For the understanding of the word, diagrams should be used as this will give clues to the meaning of the word. If it is not possible to use a diagram then try breaking the word into segments, with each segment a different colour. This will be very useful for dyslexic students, who often prefer visual presentation of information.

In terms of spelling it is important to use multisensory methods, particularly visual, to learn the correct spelling of a word.

Developing a 'schema' for Biology

"Biology is not about memory, but understanding and developing schema is a crucial element of this."

Students will be able to recall facts and details more easily if they have understood the implications of what they are learning.

Students with dyslexia may need more time to process ideas and concepts. Additionally it is important to try to reduce the memory load as much as possible, and this is where developing schema can help. A schema is essentially a set of ideas or pieces of information that can be grouped together into categories. So, for example, you may present a schema for 'flight', and the student will group together information on how and why birds are able to fly, and the different components that make this possible. These can be chunked together, which can aid recall.

Most dyslexic students will have strong visualising abilities and will be able to see the 'whole picture' and scan over it. A schema map therefore can be like a poster that incorporates the idea that is being presented and all the subsections and other related ideas. It is often more effective if students can do this themselves, but they will need a template.

As an example you can present the concept of germination (adapted from Howlett, 2001). There are many strands to this, and you can begin with a flow diagram such as flowering > water (cells swell and split testa) > photosynthesis > oxygen – respiration > growth > warmth> light. These features can all be done both in words (terms) and in pictures. It is important that the student can follow the flow of the chart and discuss each of the stages.

Taking it further

Once students have made the poster they can convert it into a mind map, with flowering as the central image and then all the offshoots. They should use as much colour as possible, and perhaps have a key to the use of colours.

Spelling in Biology

"Spelling is not always crucial, but in Biology it is!"

In Biology, a slight misspelling can mean a different word with a totally different meaning.

Taking it further

Some of the popular computer spelling programmes such as StarSpell and Wordshark can be customised to access words commonly used in Biology. This can be used for ongoing practice, but also for revision and review to find out if students have fully acquired the spelling of these words.

It is important therefore to share strategies with the student to help them understand why a word is spelled how it is, and to help them remember the spelling.

- Compile an alphabetically arranged Biology spelling book, ideally having one for each year. This can also leave scope for overlearning and reviewing, and can help the student acquire automaticity in spelling that word. It might also be a good idea to have a paper copy and the master on the computer. The student can stick the paper copy on to the back of their notebook so they can refer to these words periodically and add on any new words they come across. They can then update the master copy.
- It is also a good idea to add definitions next to the word. This can also help with recall, and of course appropriate use of the word.
- Due to the Latin and Greek roots of the words used in Biology, it can help to have a table showing singular and plural endings of Latin/Greek words (e.g. bacterium/bacteria, villus/villi, spermatazon/spermatazoa). If spaces are left, words can be added by the student as they come across them.

Labelling diagrams

"This can sometimes be quite laborious, but it is extremely important and time well spent."

Diagrams are an important part of Biology – in fact it can be described as a very visual subject. It is important that the student acquires the habit of using labels for each component of the diagram.

This is a multisensory activity, as it involves auditory, visual and tactile as well as kinaesthetic learning. It is important that constructing and drawing diagrams is not rushed and that ample time is allowed to ensure that the dyslexic student completes the diagram adequately.

Template Tease

If the student has difficulty drawing accurately, or even tracing, give them a template for the diagram but omit some pieces. This means they will have a template and be able to do most of it, and then they have to work out from the original what else they have to do. This can make the task more accessible for the dyslexic student.

The colouring of the diagram is also important, and it is crucial that the student uses a colour code for each part of the diagram. Once they run out of colours they can start to do shading and stripes.

Howlett (2001) suggests that there should always be a main label, and that labels should ideally be written horizontally and not clutter up the diagram – they should be able to be read as easily as possible in a radiating pattern, rather than at conflicting angles, so the eye can most easily glance along them without distraction.

Taking it further

If students want to use the iPad for this there are apps they can use for drawing. They should be able to do the colour-coding and print out the result in colour. This is quite important, as often the handwriting of students with dyslexia is not very legible. Students should work in small groups for this – perhaps two or three students, but not more.

Making connections in Biology

"We are always looking for common themes and strands across the curriculum, and we need to strive to do this in Biology."

There is now growing research to indicate the importance of making connections across the curriculum for effective learning.

Taking it further

The student can develop this activity by making a mind map to show links between subjects. This can link Biology to PE, as shown, but also to other subjects – History (famous sportspeople), Geography (terrain, environment, orienteering, walking, etc.) This can make the links as wide as possible. Try to get the student to think outside the box.

The quality of the connections the student makes are important for effective learning.

Most students utilise three elements in learning – rehearsal, elaboration and organisation. Elaboration should include the ability to summarise, then organisation to construct connections and develop relationships between ideas. Organisation of ideas is the crux of making cross-curricular transfer and relevant connections. Classification into categories is a major learning feature, and subjects such as Biology lend themselves to this, as most of the topics are classified for easy access and recognition.

It is important that the student with dyslexia is assisted in the organisation of ideas and concepts, and helped to identify connections across the curriculum. We also need to acknowledge, as cognitive science indicates, that students' previous knowledge (personal and cultural experiences) can influence how they organise and link new information.

Link with PE

The students learn about the similarities and differences between aerobic cellular respiration and anaerobic fermentation during different types of athletic activity. They learn about different muscles and organs such as heart and lungs. They can then link this with PE and encouraged to make a table with headings for 'Activity', 'What it does' and 'Principles that relate to Biology'.

Additional language learning

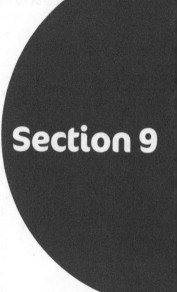

Using graphic organisers for the bigger picture

"We recognise that some second-language learners can be dyslexic, and we spend time ensuring that their needs are met."

We are living in multicultural and multi-linguistic societies, and this diversity needs to be reflected in educational practice.

Taking it further

The students could make an idea matrix. This involves using paper with large squares like a timetable, but instead of inserting classes they can draw an image to represent an idea. They can have an idea for every subject and then a glossary on the next page explaining the importance of the idea. This can be totally open-ended to give the student as much scope as possible.

It is important that bi/multilingual students are adequately assessed for dyslexia. This section looks at strategies for supporting dyslexic students for whom English is an additional language(EAL).

EAL students who are dyslexic will very likely respond to visual strategies and need as much visual input as possible, so graphic organisers can be excellent. It is important however that this is complemented by text, as the need to see the word or phrase as well as a visual is important. It is also important to recognise different cultures as much as possible.

A graphic organiser is a visual representation of conceptual knowledge. It can relate to facts as well as ideas. It can help English language learners remember and understand the content of the information they are learning, and also reduce the linguistic demands placed on them.

Examples of commonly used graphic organisers include comparison and contrast diagrams, spidergrams, cause and effect maps, time ladder or sequence maps, and flow charts. These are all useful for dyslexic students.

- Select the type of organiser you want the students to use.
- Select a concept/phrase or word to be learned.
- Allow the student to complete the image.
- Get the student to select other concepts or ideas themselves.

Games to consolidate reading

"Even at secondary level, games are the only way for many dyslexic students."

Games can be especially good for EAL students, as they are quite non-threatening.

Although games can be competitive, they do not always have to be. However, it is crucial to incorporate a fun element into these. This can be an activity that students do in groups, and the social interchange can be particularly helpful for dyslexic students.

There is a wide range of games available: quizzes, word games, puzzles, proverbs, slang expressions, anagrams, random-sentence generators and computer-assisted language-learning activities. This activity can encourage students to access and understand narrative texts.

- Introduce the story to the students – they should already be familiar with it. You need to appoint a panel of judges – try three students.
- The students should identify the main part of the story, including the plot and characters.
- Then the game starts. In teams students must write down all the contrasts they can find in the story, including the characters.
- They should then look at the similarities in different parts of the book, including the characters.
- This encourages students to build connections and draw conclusions about what they are reading.

For this activity, the students can draw two overlapping circles on a piece of paper, and list the differences in the outer circles and the similarities in the intersection (a Venn diagram). They should then discuss the results, and the judges can give comments and marks.

Taking it further

Have a look at the following website http://a4esl.org, which has bilingual quizzes for most languages including Arabic–English, Spanish–English and Italian–English. There is also a range of games: http://www.manythings.org/vocabulary/games/a/

See also Crossbow Education's *Getting it Right for Dyslexic Learners: the Complete Toolkit* by Beccie Hawes (2016), and also Pot the Lobster, a language game that can be suitable for secondary bilingual students: http://www.crossboweducation.com

Combining listening and reading

"Audiobooks are ideal for EAL students – they can play them as many times as they wish."

When listening to audiobooks, it is best if the students have a task or tasks to complete. Choose a good-quality recording.

There is an opportunity here to introduce the student to the metacognitive cycle – and develop higher-order learning concepts and autonomy in learning. It is important that metacognitive strategies are not overlooked for EAL students. To remind you, the metacognitive cycle is as follows:

- Self-questioning
- Self-clarifying
- Self-understanding
- Self-direction
- Self-monitoring
- Self-assessment.

Students should also be encouraged to note the key chapters and play these again. It is also a good idea for the student to have a printed copy of the book in front of them at the same time. Certainly this should be encouraged for the first few readings.

Build up a bank of audiobooks read by people with different accents. If you can find a book with an accent in a student's first language, that can be useful.

- Encourage the student to choose a book.
- Discuss the book with the student – the plot (brief outline), key characters, context/location, time span, etc.
- You may want to do some paired reading to get the student into the book.
- Depending on the ability of the student, see if they can read the book without the voice recording to begin with. Try one or two chapters.
- Now get the student to listen to the recording one chapter at a time.
- After each chapter the student should complete some questions that you provide for them.
- Give the student the questions to refer to when they first play the audiobook.
- Questions should follow each chapter.
- After several readings with the text, the student should listen to the text without the book.
- Finally they should read the book in print only.

The ROAR technique – repetition, overlearning and review

"I would go with the ROAR technique every time! This is ideal for EAL students."

It is well established that overlearning is essential for learners with dyslexia – and even more so for EAL learners, as they need a great deal of reinforcement.

The key point about overlearning is that it must be varied as much as possible; although it requires repetition, this should involve a range of different kind of activities. It is the same word/idea/concept that should be focused on.

- Identify the word or idea that you want the student to overlearn.
- Teach this using a visual technique in the first instance, as this is likely to be the student's learning style, especially if they are an EAL student.
- Repetition should also involve another visual strategy, but get the student to do this themselves.
- Then the student can engage in an auditory strategy – talking or reading.
- It is a good idea if the student can discuss this with you or a small group in the class.
- This should be done a number of times; this is where the overlearning comes in.
- Next you should get the student to practise this as much as possible over the next few weeks.
- Review – this will indicate whether the strategy has been successful or if the student requires more overlearning.

Taking it further

It is a good idea if the student develops a chart for themselves, to record the idea, the strategies used and how successful they were.

Learning language through culture – the multi-literacies

"Culture is one of the factors to hang on to, and it is also important to recognise the multi-literacy idea. "

It is important that the school is culture-rich and that the materials and resources available are culturally appropriate.

Teaching tip

Diniz (2002) suggests that teachers need to be able to differentiate between cognitive and cultural issues in relation to difficulties in literacy at the classroom level in order to support students' literacy learning in the most appropriate ways.

There is considerable evidence that programmes designed to address literacy difficulties also need to take into account the fact that cultural factors need to be considered (Wearmouth, Soler and Reid, 2003).

If you accept the notion of multi-literacies (Wearmouth et al. 2001), it is no longer possible to develop one universal programme to address the range of barriers to literacy. This also implies that schools need to adopt a multi-disciplinary approach to investigating and teaching literacy.

Multi-literacy implies that students use a number of different literacy paradigms – e.g. home language, school language, language used with peer group, etc. It is important to be aware of this when teaching EAL students.

- Take note of the language students use when talking in groups, particularly the EAL students.
- See if any of the words/phrases or ideas are different from what you might expect.
- Note any cultural differences between groups in the class.

Taking it further

You can get the students to do this activity themselves. Ask them to note down the phrases they use with friends that they would not use in class! This might be a bit tricky, but you can give them some guidance here.

This emphasises that it is important for EAL students to work in groups with others from similar cultures for some of the time. Clearly it is also important that they adapt to different cultures in the class. However, as a teacher of EAL students you need to recognise the notion of multi-literacies and how this impacts literacy at school.

Keeping instructions short and clear

"This is a simple point, yet such an important one."

Instructions need to be kept short due to difficulties with working memory, which means that students with dyslexia can only hold one instruction at a time in their head. You need to ensure that each instruction has been understood before moving on.

This is a fundamental point that applies to all students with dyslexia. Try also to ensure that you use the right level of vocabulary for the students – for example instead of the word 'imminent' you would prefer 'soon'.

- Look at all the instructions on a worksheet or set of teaching materials.
- Can the sentences be made shorter? For example:

'I want you to select two points from the list below that highlight an appropriate response to the main question asked in the passage.'

Changes that can be made:

- Read the passage again – give title of passage.
- Write down the main point – we discussed this in class – clue (give a clue).
- Choose two points from below – (you then present the list) that can have some connection with this point.
- Can you then write a sentence to show why you think your answer is correct?

You can see in the second version that the single sentence has been divided into four different short tasks.

It is important to review worksheets before giving them to students to ensure that the instructions are short and clear.

Taking it further

Once the EAL student has completed the worksheet, ask them what – if anything – they found difficult in relation to understanding the task. You can ask them if they have any suggestions for improvements.

MSE – multisensory, structured and explicit

"This is great for teaching students with dyslexia, and I would certainly ensure this is used for all EAL students with dyslexia."

Taking it further

This type of activity can be shared by all subject teachers. It is important that this is part of professional development, as all teachers will be giving EAL students instructions and worksheets. Ensure they use MSE strategies!

Multisensory teaching and learning is key when teaching students with dyslexia. and is important for EAL students who may need more time to achieve automaticity, depending on their level of language. They will require overlearning.

Activity

M = Multisensory – This is the planning part of teaching. You need to gather as many multisensory strategies and materials as possible. For example:

Auditory – make lists, find out information

Visual – drawings, diagrams, DVDs, apps

Kinaesthetic – visits, field trips, activities

Persistent – lengthy tasks, problem-solving activities

Global – overview, short tasks, frequent breaks, discussion

Social – work in groups and pairs, discussion

Metacognitive – problem solving, thinking skills

Tactile – hands on, model making, deomstration

S = Structured – This is very important for students with dyslexia; tasks should be in clear steps, They can even be numbered.

E = Explicit – Do not leave any room for doubt or choice. Try to be clear at least until the student has mastered the concept. Then you can give choices that can in fact lead to desirable outcomes such as developing higher-order concepts and transferring learning.

Physical
Education

Section 10

Team building for self-esteem

"My job is to make sure that even if they do not excel at sport they still embrace it – this is important for self-esteem."

Physical Education has the potential to be an excellent team builder. This can be a real bonus for students with dyslexia, but it is important that they feel part of the group.

Taking it further

It is a good idea to explain to the class why people have different attributes and attitudes to sport. This can couple with . the notion of diversity and acceptance of others. This can be a valuable exercise for all students.

Some dyslexic students are fortunate and easily slip into the Physical Education mould, but for others it can more difficult. It is important that these students receive additional support so that Physical Education is a positive experience for them. There are a number of strategies that can be used.

There is risk attached to allowing students to select their own teams for games. In each team ir is important to have a 'team builder', who:

- is a good listener
- is not too competitive – able to share
- encourages others
- gives appropriate feedback
- is respected by their peer group.

Ensure that students with dyslexia – particularly those who are lacking in confidence – are teamed with a team builder.

For example the 'can't do it but let's have fun anyway' student wants to have fun and can think of light-hearted aspects of the game. This can support the student who finds it challenging, by helping them fit into the group and feel more comfortable.

You may want to look at real sports personalities –past and present and get the class to look at the specific attributes of these people.

Ball games for confidence and coordination

"Some students with dyslexia can experience motor coordination problems. This will clearly have a major impact on their ability to participate in ball games and other sports."

Dyslexic student may have poor hand–eye coordination or perceptual difficulties, which affect their skills in sports.

It needs to be recognised that quite a number of students with dyslexia can excel at sport. There are many examples of people with dyslexia who have excelled in football, rugby, athletics, motor racing, fencing and swimming.

Things to remember

When arranging ball games and other similar games, it is important to remember some key points in relation to the challenges that some students with dyslexia can face in PE.

Challenges include:

- Difficulty with motor control.
- Clumsiness – dropping things, etc.
- Poor hand–eye coordination.
- Forgetting the sequence in games and activities.
- Losing track of the ball in ball games.
- Misinterpreting rules.
- Poor directional awareness.
- Needing more time to think things through.
- Short-term memory issues.

Practise ball control

This it helps prevent the student from being thrown in at the deep end. They need a lot of structured practice – preferably with one other person – in throwing and catching the ball. Start with a larger ball and move on to smaller balls.

Computer games can help develop fine motor control as well as hand–eye coordination.

Teaching tip

You can utilise the principles of peer tutoring/reciprocal learning here. The main point of this is that both students in a pair teach each other, and take turns at being the teacher. This can be a good confidence builder for the student with dyslexia. You can also encourage them to use multisensory strategies after explaining to them what these are.

Skip to success

"There is a link between reading and exercise, and skipping can be that link!"

There have been quite a number of theories linking exercise with reading, and there are many scientific and psychological factors responsible for this.

Taking it further

Once students have mastered the technique you can then extend this to make it a class competition – which they can join in fully. You can also extend it to other coordination activities such as using a hula hoop, which is somewhat similar to skipping.

Essentially most exercise involves the whole brain, and it can therefore be good for linking the left and right hemispheres, making learning more holistic. This can in turn have a beneficial effect on reading, which is essentially a holistic activity. Additionally, exercise can make the student feel refreshed and relaxed.

Skipping is only one such activity that can have a beneficial effect, but it also utilises hand–eye–foot coordination, and this can be excellent practice for students with dyslexia.

Students should first practise jumping over a low hurdle, which should be positioned at about the same height as a skipping rope might be during skipping. They should do this a number of times in order to get the feel of the height and therefore achieve a degree of automaticity.

Students then start by using a coloured skipping rope if possible – they should choose the colour. This can help them to see it when they are skipping at speed.

Start with fairly modest targets – e.g. five skips, then rest. You should then increase the figure by two skips each time.

Eventually the students will be able to set themselves targets of how many skips they can manage without tripping. Try to make this into a game.

Equipment checklist

"Developing this type of checklist can become part of the routine for the dyslexic student; it is very valuable, as they can otherwise confuse and forget equipment."

It is important to help dyslexic students with organisation and planning. In secondary school in particular there may be a lot of equipment and materials to remember to bring every day.

Material to remember every day could include ruler, timetable, books, pens, pencils, highlighters, paper – plain and ruled – PE kit, materials for specialist subjects like Music, Food Technology and Art, and food and drink for break times. This can cause difficulties and considerable stress, and so the student will need some support to ensure that they bring all the necessary equipment each day. This idea focuses on PE, but it can be used for other subjects also.

Get the student to make up a chart using lined paper, with three columns. One column will show the equipment, another will have a space for a comment that may refer to something particular about that item, and the third column will have space for a tick when the item has been remembered. One item should be shown per line.

Bonus Idea ★

Keep the to do list in check!!

It is too easy to compile a massive to do list and realistically not being able to accomplish the tasks in the list. One way to overcome this is to be as specific as possible in the to do list and that way even if you have only carried out some off the tasks in a category at least you can tick them off the list. Try not to have any more than four to six points in any one list and try to complete this before compiling another list!

Taking it further

If there are a lot of remarks in the comment column, the student can then make a 'to do' list underneath the equipment checklist.

Organising and locating equipment

"I spend quite a bit of time at the beginning of term going over the names of all the equipment and indicating what they are for. This pays off especially for students with dyslexia, but it benefits everyone."

Physical Education does require a considerable amount of equipment, often with specific names. This can present a challenge for the student with dyslexia, as they can easily confuse these names and forget the purpose of different pieces of equipment.

It is useful to go over all the equipment they are likely to use in the year. This can be useful even if they are not using it immediately but means it will not be totally new to them.

Knowing and retaining information about the equipment can be challenging for dyslexic students. They need to devise a strategy for knowing what the equipment does and when they will be using it.

- Discuss all the equipment with the class – showing them the equipment and demonstrating how it should be used.
- Get each student to take a photo of all the equipment that can be used in PE.
- Get them to write a list of all the purposes the equipment can be used for.
- Print both on to separate A4 sheets – use as many sheets as possible.
- Get the student to cut the images and lists out and stick them in their notebook. (Initially the student should place them in position and wait for you to confirm this is correct.)
- Finally, in pairs, they should cover up each of the descriptions and indicate to their partner what equipment the picture shows. until they get them all right.

Yoga and meditation

"Yoga has a profoundly positive effect on all students academically, emotionally and socially' – Charlotta Martinus, founder of Teen Yoga

Yoga is without doubt a calming activity. It can also be part of a healthy school initiative, as yoga is a whole-body intervention – with diet, exercise and relaxation all built into one.

There is now increasing interest in yoga in schools (for example, the book *Once Upon a Pose* by Donna Freeman).

It is important to have a structured programme so the student can see what they have done. Yoga practice should be a whole-body and mind experience.

Everyone can do yoga, so it is good for the student with dyslexia as they will feel included; it encourages collaboration.

One of the additional benefits of yoga is that the students also get to accept silence and harness it. The relaxation at the end helps the students to clear their minds and to practise calmness. This can set the students up for the day – or, if carried out later in the day, can send them home more relaxed.

Yoga in class

Yoga activities can also be integrated into PE.

- Starting the students off in pairs can be fun, and makes them feel less inhibited.
- It is also a good idea to give a brief introduction to the background of yoga so they get a sense of the purpose of the positions.
- It is important that they understand the whole-body aspect, and the lifestyle of a yogi. However, you must emphasise that they only do this according to their own capabilities and how they feel. It is not a competition, and there is no such thing as failure!

Teaching tip

It is important to have a fully trained and accredited instructor to carry out the yoga classes, as injuries can happen if the students are not properly supervised. It is important that the yoga positions are done properly and gradually.

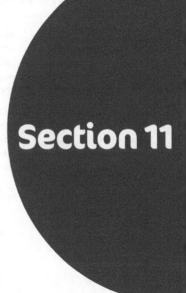

Food Technology and Textiles (Home Economics)

Section 11

Planning the kitchen

"This is a good way to help the student with dyslexia practise planning and organising skills. It is also non-threatening and fun!"

It is well accepted that students with dyslexia have difficulty with planning and organisation. This is certainly the case with essays and written work in general, but it can also be the case with other subjects such as Food Technology.

Many foods have similar-sounding names and some may be strange to the student. Other problems may include locating where the ingredients and utensils are kept, and planning the kitchen for easy access.

Essentially this can be a visual task, and it should be one that the student with dyslexia can tackle with some ease. However, often they need to be guided and supported to be able to do this.

- Emphasise to the student that the only items on the counter will be items you intend to use that day (as long as they are not perishable foods, as they need to be in the fridge). The slogan: No counter clutter!
- You now need to get the student to note down all the items that will go into the kitchen. This can be a formidable list, but try to get them to use categories:
  - cooking and microwave utensils
  - herbs and spices, etc.
- Now get them to draw an outline of the kitchen – start with a square kitchen.
- Next they should show the cupboards and sink, and position the fridge and cooker.
- They can now place the items using a key – a number or colour key would work.
- They can pair up and discuss each kitchen with the other person, and make any changes that might arise from this discussion.

Taking it further

Students could make a model of the kitchen in Art. They can team up for this, as it can be a major project – they might even do this in groups of four.

Finally they can write a paragraph indicating why they think their kitchen has a good plan.

Planning the menu – know the food

"This can be great fun for the dyslexic student, and they can be very inventive – it is important to give them that opportunity to be creative."

There are two aspects to this – knowing the food, and planning the menu to ensure that the meals are well balanced.

It is important to remember that many celebrity chefs, like Jamie Oliver, are dyslexic. He is certainly the most famous, but many adults with dyslexia enter the hospitality industry and carve out a superb career for themselves. They combine their skills at working in teams with creativity and can fit in well.

However, at secondary school there can be barriers. There are so many different foods, often with strange-sounding names, that even identifying the foods can be challenging. Students with dyslexia may also have difficulty remembering which foods have which nutritional values and in what category they belong. This is something they need to be familiar with so they can plan a well-balanced menu containing a wide range of nutrients.

The first step is to identify an ingredient by general category. They can do this in a table, for example, in which they paste pictures of the foods. This is important, as they need to see what the food looks like. The table might be organised into three columns: Classification (e.g. Carbohydrate), Examples (e.g. Vegetables, legumes, whole grains, fruit, nuts), Preparation (e.g. Usually eaten fresh, but may be boiled or heated).

Taking it further

Students could plan a menu for a week. This needs to be a visual menu – use colours and pictures for each day and each food item. They must remember to make it balanced. At the end they should write a paragraph explaining how they have achieved this balance.

Measuring and weighing

"Food Technology activities tend to be cross-curricular, as they involve some Maths, and also Science. They are good for dyslexic students as they involve lots of hands-on action."

Food Technology – particularly the practical element – can involve a great deal of multitasking.

Taking it further

Students could make a giant poster for the wall using graphics for all the measures they will need.

It is possible to buy this type of poster, but it is better for the students to make their own.

This can make it exciting and interesting for the student. It is important that students with dyslexia acquire a degree of automaticity in the various terminology and the calculations involved in weighing and measuring ingredients. There are symbols, new concepts and vocabulary all of which can be challenging for the student with dyslexia.

Just how confusing this can be is shown below:

- 3 teaspoons (tsp) = 1 tablespoon (tbsp)
- 4 tbsp = ¼ cup
- 1 tbsp = ½ fluid ounce (fl oz)
- 1 pound (lb) = 453.5 grams (g)
- 1 oz = 28 g/30 millilitres (mL).

It is important to make these measures dyslexia friendly in such a way that the student can access this information quickly. When they are preparing food they may not have time to check up on these measures.

You need to translate all the abbreviations, numbers and conversions they will need into graphics. Additionally, you can use coloured measuring spoons.

The student can draw a chart with an image of spoons and cups – they can make a mark in the cup for half-full, one-third, etc. In this way, instead of using fractions and numbers to measure, they can use graphics.

Sew good – strategies for sewing and knitting

"This is another excellent cross-curricular activity; it is hands-on and practical, and can involve creativity too – students with dyslexia can really enjoy this subject."

Once students have mastered the basics they can find textiles really enjoyable. This can also be a good outlet for creativity.

However, there are a number of challenges and hurdles they must first overcome. For example, in knitting there is almost a new language – knit and purl, special stitches...and of course knitting patterns are not always dyslexia friendly. Words are often close together, and there will be only a few visuals along the way.

The use of visuals is essential for students with dyslexia carrying out these kind of craft activities. There are a number of ways of introducing visuals – you can use highlighters like flags to indicate where you start a new row or a different part of the pattern.

You can also make a knitting chart with one colour of highlighter for knit rows and a different colour for purl rows. Use a sticky note to mark the line being worked on.

It is also a good idea to photocopy an enlarged image of the pattern so that it will be easier to see, as patterns are often quite small.

It may help the student to articulate what they are doing while knitting, for example 'knit one, yarn over, knit two together, knit one, yarn over ...' and so on. The auditory/spoken stimulus may help the student stay on track.

Read through the pattern before starting to make sure the student understands it. Ask the student to try to visualise the finished product in pairs.

Taking it further

Get the students to work in small groups and together rewrite the pattern in their own words. They can use counters instead of the actual numbers to make it more visual. This will really build their confidence!

Service delivery – hosting the dinner

"This is kitchen drama at its best, and a real confidence booster for the student with dyslexia."

Serving and hosting a dinner is a great planning activity, and the icing on the cake after a lot of hard work and preparation.

Taking it further

If we are to be fully multisensory then we need to incorporate taste. The students can make up an additional table to record taste. They can make up a list of the foods they are serving and score them on a scale – something like 5 = absolutely marvellous, while 1 = no thanks! At the end they can compare what they think with the guests who were served the dinner.

It is important that the reality of serving up matches and justifies the long, hard preparation that has gone into preparation.

Serving and hosting a dinner does require a great deal of planning, so it is best done in teams. It is important that each member of the team has a job to do. There can be a lot of different tasks associated with this, such as food preparation, cooking and monitoring progress, preparing and setting the table, serving, and then clearing up. It can be a really fun activity, but it can also be stressful – a lot of things are happening at the same time. However, it is excellent practice in management, planning and multitasking.

It is important that plans are prepared well in advance. They should include a 'time' plan, and the group should also be familiar with the cooking appliances – e.g. oven/hob space, mini oven, grill and microwave, and how they are to be used. This can be written up in the form of a table.

The team will also need to plan the timings for when to prepare the different courses, i.e. starter, main course, side dishes and dessert. These all need to be worked out in advance.

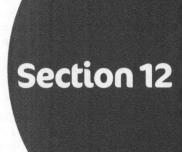

Self-esteem and motivation

Lots of circle time

"I would never have thought circle time would work so well with secondary students, but it does!"

Circle time is very popular with primary children, and is used widely. Less is known about its use in secondary school, probably because it does not easily fit into a curriculum subject.

Circle time usually gets a slot in a 'form' class or in 'life skills'. These, however, are not core subjects and circle time can often be a forgotten area. It does serve a useful purpose for all students, but can be particularly beneficial for students who are dyslexic, providing a significant boost to self-esteem. More than that, though, it can help the whole class become more aware of differences and diversity. It promotes self-awareness and awareness of the needs of others.

This activity can be done either with the whole class or by dividing the class into groups. It is best to start with pairs, though; each pair can work on their own and then join the whole class.

Each has to say something positive about the other. They should write this down. Then each has to say how they think others see them. They should make a list using people they come into contact with regularly, e.g. brothers/ sisters, parents, teachers, friends, school staff...and the partner they are working with. Then they should discuss this with their partner and say why they think like that.

The idea of this activity is to help students actually think about others in their life, and that it matters what they think about them and vice versa. It will also help for them to share this with another member of the class, and to reflect on this.

Empowering the learner – intrinsic motivation

"Surely the aim is to help the learner help themselves."

It is often the case that students with dyslexia are over-supported.

They do need support, and they need a structure too. But it is important that they are also encouraged to develop self–sufficiency and become more in control of their own learning. Having this control and independence can help with confidence, self-esteem and developing intrinsic motivation, and makes them a more effective lifelong learner.

Essentially there are two aspects to motivation – one is extrinsic (reward) and the other is intrinsic (internal or self-motivation). We may need to start with extrinsic motivation so that there is a tangible reward for doing something, but eventually you need to switch to intrinsic motivation, which is the key to learning independently.

To achieve this, however, the learner needs to have a desired goal and some determination to succeed. Children who experience barriers to learning, such as those with dyspraxia and dyslexia, can find motivation challenging, as repeated failure will result in serious demotivation. In fact this state is often referred to as 'learned helplessness'. It is crucial that the learner does not reach this state, and for that reason early success is important when tackling new tasks. It is also important that both extrinsic and intrinsic motivation are taken into account in the planning of learning.

Considering the students who are dyslexic, make a list of the potential intrinsic motivating features that you can utilise when working with them.

Teaching tip

For intrinsic motivation learners need to understand what they are learning, to be inquisitive, and to be able to see the new learning as part of a bigger picture – for example, a child may say 'I want to learn to swim because I want to use a kayak.' This child would be intrinsically motivated to learn to swim as they see the benefits of being able to do this.

Taking it further

One of the skills in teaching is being able to recognise a learner's natural motivators. Often learners may not be aware of this, and it is the teacher who has to recognise it and help the students use their natural skills and resources. Try to identify the natural strengths in your dyslexic students that can be used to encourage intrinsic motivation.

Motivation though feedback

"I never really appreciated the impact feedback could have until I saw the difference it made to my dyslexic students."

Every learner benefits from feedback to ensure they are on the correct path. But feedback is essential for learners who are dyslexic.

Taking it further

You can get the student to suggest themselves how they can improve – this is a practice that is becoming increasingly popular for end-of-year school reports where students are able to comment on how they can improve.

It is also important that feedback is handled properly because it can lead to the learner becoming intrinsically motivated (see Idea 81).

Golden Rule 1 – start with the positive

Feedback should be continuous and formative and it should not necessarily come at the end of a task. It should be positive or framed positively, to avoid demotivating the student.

Golden Rule 2 – say thank you for doing this

Even comments like 'thanks for handing this in to me' are positive. This might seem condescending, but for some dyslexic students submitting work on completion can be quite an ordeal.

Golden Rule 3 – be suggestive, not directive

Make suggestions rather than issue directives – 'Perhaps this might sound better' or 'Have you thought of doing this?' What the student has done is okay, but this other approach might be better.

Golden Rule 4 – give examples

They to avoid making general statements about work; be specific and give examples so dyslexic student will be able to refer back to this.

Golden Rule 5 – show progress

Indicate to the student that they have made some progress. Remember that small points to you might be big points to the student.

Motivation through independence and success

"It is a well-used phrase but nothing breeds success like success, and helping the dyslexic student become an independent learner is part of that process."

It is important to encourage dyslexic students to develop an understanding of the learning process and how they can become more effective learners through tackling problems independently.

It is almost automatic for some dyslexic students to ask someone if they cannot readily find the answer. Others of course may hide and be quite embarrassed – either way we need to help them develop independent processing skills so they can do it themselves. This can not only lead to independent learning, but also to intrinsic motivation (see Idea 81).

It is important that students with dyslexia break out of the dependency culture as early as possible.

In a part of the classroom place a poster on the wall indicating that this is a 'no hands up zone'. Decorate the poster to indicate that the zone is a thinking zone, and that no questions are allowed.

You can get the students themselves to draw posters showing that it is a 'no hands up zone', and ask them to indicate *why* it is this type of zone. The emphasis is on thinking skills and on the students working things out for themselves. Once this is done you are ready to try it out. Try it first with a mixed group, including at least one dyslexic student.

Evaluate how it works and make adjustments as necessary. It is a good idea to allow them in the zone for only a short period – e.g. 30 minutes maximum – to begin with.

Taking it further

Follow-up activities can include selecting a 'no hands up champion' – the student who scores the most points. All students start with 20 points and these are reduced each time they ask a question during the week. It is important not to discourage students from asking questions in class, but you should emphasise that questions are not permitted while working in the zone.

The motivating environment

"I now realise that the environment can be a key motivational factor in learning."

The environment can have a considerable impact on learning, and especially so for the dyslexic student.

Take it Further

From the results of the audit you can now record the following:

- Aspects I am happy with
- Aspects I would like to change but will find it difficult to do
- It would be difficult to change because
- Aspects I do intend to change
- Changes to be made to the learning environment:

Environmental preferences are very individual, However there are some points that apply to most dyslexic students. For example, they usually prefer space and not being crowded together, comfortable chairs making the environment quite informal, being able to move about the room, colour and light are important, and background music can also help. They also need a structure and routine, so the classroom should have some formality in that the student will know where particular materials are to be found. Monitor the extent to which you are able to accommodate environmental preferences as a motivating factor.

1. Furniture

Student Chairs	Tick	Comment
Teachers desk	"	"
Desk flexibility		

2. Colour and design

Colours	Tick	Comment
Amount of light	"	"
Desk flexibility		
Visually appealing		

3. Classroom routines

Predictability	Tick	Comment
Structure	"	"
Choice		
Opportunities for exploring		
Promotes interest		
Stress-free		

Staff
development

Section 13

Learning styles across the curriculum

"I think this is the key – the whole school approach!"

Teachers need to develop appropriate learning tools, strategies, methods and materials to help students succeed.

Teaching tip

It is crucial that factors associated with learning style are taken into consideration in planning and in assessment.

Learning styles are best adopted as a whole-school approach. The key points are the learning environment, the connections between new learning and previous learning, activities, and the big picture – a global overview of the topic.

- The classroom design and layout should accommodate features such as colour, sound and music and design.
- Some learning environments may be more suited to left-hemisphere learners, others to right-hemisphere learners.
- Environmental preferences can be considered following discussion with learners or through observation of learners in different settings.

It is important to acknowledge that learning styles can overlap and complement other aspects of learning such as multiple intelligences, metacognition and thinking and teaching styles, and these can lend themselves to whole-school cross-curricular initiatives.

- The cognitive dimension includes modality preferences, attention, memory processes and concept development.
- The affective dimension includes personality variables that influence learning, such as persistence and perseverance, frustration, reaction to reinforcement, personal interests, etc.
- The physiological dimension includes time-of-day rhythms, the need for mobility and environmental elements.

Taking it further

You can take a subject-by-subject approach where each subject teacher works out how they can accommodate learning styles in their own subject.

Developing and using an audit

"A whole-school audit is always insightful."

It is important to obtain an awareness of the understanding of the school staff in relation to dyslexia.

Circulate the following to the school staff: Students with dyslexia require accommodations in every subject. The idea of this audit is to find out how you manage these and what challenges you experience in supporting dyslexic students.

- Have you considered individual learning styles? Please give details.
- How do you cater for thinking skills in the curriculum?
- How can you raise the self-esteem of students with dyslexia? Can we do more?
- How do we deal with motivation for students with dyslexia at the classroom level, the school level and at home?
- Have you considered the importance of music and exercise for learning?
- Is there music in the classrooms, corridor or recreation areas?
- Is there free space dedicated to parents and to students for their own purposes?
- Is the entrance to the school visually appealing?
- Is there a whole-school policy on emotional literacy?
- How are the emotional and social needs of the staff catered for?
- Is there evidence in the corridors, school handbook, wall displays and in the classrooms that the school recognises diversity?
- Do parents feel a sense of ownership within the school? How are they made to feel part of it?

Teaching tip

This can provide important base-line information that can guide staff development. It can also inform the learning support staff about how they can assist various departments. Take the audit beyond simply asking about awareness of dyslexia to work out how the school as a whole can deal more effectively with students with dyslexia.

Taking it further

You can make a single statement for all staff when summarising the results.

- The supports we use for students with dyslexia.
- Other supports we can consider.
- Type of school climate and ethos we want to achieve as a school.
- How this can be achieved.

Follow through – making the most of training

"Professional development is always useful, but the follow-up is more important."

There is an increasing awareness now of dyslexia, and we find that schools — and particularly secondary schools — are requesting staff development.

Taking it further

It is important to have a coordinated plan for staff development.

A follow-up discussion session is important, and should take place a few weeks after so that staff have had time to discuss any implications. Each department can prepare some feedback on how they support students with dyslexia and present this to all staff.

Subject teachers should consider the following:

- What is my current understanding of dyslexia?
- How has that changed following this course/talk?
- How do I support students with dyslexia now?
- How can I change this after the talk?
- What type of support should I seek from the learning support staff?

Things they may also consider include:

- using coloured pens
- using bullet points for notes
- encouraging students to read a daily newspaper
- taking time – get it right
- getting students to use a laptop in class
- encouraging self-belief
- focusing on content, not spelling or grammar
- helping students know their strengths and deal with their weaknesses
- allowing students to use the internet to research (easier to read on a computer screen than in books)
- split a problem up using a spider diagram to aid understanding
- encourage students to read magazines they enjoy; it is the reading that is important
- get students to plan work before writing
- encourage them to think positively and have a can-do attitude.

**Preparing
to leave**

Section 14

Choosing a course/career

"I am convinced there should be more of this at school – career choice is such an important matter."

There can be such a confusing array of courses, universities and careers to choose from that this can be a very challenging and stressful area for the student with dyslexia.

Teaching tip

In no way should the student with dyslexia undersell themselves. They need to aim high – and with encouragement, they can do this. They need sound advice as soon as possible to be in a position to do this.

There is always the question of qualifications and grades, and the student may want to shop around to get the right university to match the grades they expect to get.

You can ask some of your students what kind of concerns they experience. We have done that, and some examples are shown below.

What type of work will I be able to do?
The short answer to that is simple – anything! If the young person has, for example, an interest in journalism, medicine, law or accountancy then with support they can achieve that ambition. Certain occupations can be more challenging because of, and indeed depending on, the nature of the dyslexic difficulties, but no occupation should necessarily be ruled out.

Every profession, no matter how dyslexia friendly, might well contain some elements or tasks that can prove difficult for a dyslexic person. But the important point is that the dyslexic person is not barred from any occupation because of their dyslexia. Also, it is generally possible to work out accommodations, preferably with the support of the employer, to support the dyslexic person in the workplace.

Are there any professions /occupations that should be avoided?

Some professions, such as medicine and law, may have demanding entry qualifications

Taking it further

Self-help is usually the best type of help, as the student has control over this. Each dyslexic person is different, and therefore the most effective way to deal with any challenging situation is on an individual basis. It can also be best if the young person with dyslexia takes the lead.

for training, but this should not prevent the young person from applying for these courses – they will be supported if they receive a place. University tutors on these courses are increasingly gaining experience in dealing with dyslexic students, becoming more aware of what dyslexia is and more knowledgeable about the type of support required for both practical and theoretical work.

Will I be supported on a college or university course?

The simple answer is yes! Most countries have legislation to support all students with a recognised disability, and dyslexia is certainly recognised in terms of legislation as a disability.

Most universities have guidance for students with dyslexia, or even those who suspect they might have dyslexia but have not yet been diagnosed. This guidance can normally be accessed via the university website or the student services department.

Should I declare my dyslexia on my application forms?

The correct and appropriate answer to that question is yes, and we always suggest that a dyslexic person does declare their dyslexia on their application form. Legally this should not result in discrimination against them, and it informs the prospective college and employer at the outset so that they will be made aware of the accommodations that will have to be made.

Transition to university – golden rules

"This is such an important step for the student with dyslexia – it has to be carefully handled."

All transitions can be challenging for students with dyslexia, but perhaps the one from school to university is most crucial.

Teaching tip

Ensure liaison at a professional level – it is important that the school management, teachers and the students themselves can link with the universities in the area at an early stage. Visits and excursions to the university are essential. Parental involvement is also desirable, although it is important that the students take initiative themselves.

There are some golden rules for helping the student through this process.

- **Develop independence** – It is important to help the student become more independent in study long before this transition occurs. Give them opportunities to develop their own study techniques.
- **Develop confidence** – This is so important at university as students with dyslexia. They will come up against students for whom study is relatively straightforward, and it is important that they do not feel undermined by this. Highlight the positive aspects of dyslexia and help them to believe in themselves.
- **Make full use of accommodations** – It is important to emphasise that the accommodations dyslexic students receive are merely levelling the playing field and should be fully accessed.
- **Foster positivity** – It can be very exciting starting university, and it is important that the student feels this and is not too apprehensive about the transition. It is a good idea to set up support groups for students with dyslexia.
- **Develop maturity** – The system should promote maturity by providing students with responsibilities. They will become more confident if they have experienced responsibility.
- **Help to develop social confidence** – This is a school responsibility, as school is a social organisation.

Taking it further

The students with dyslexia could set up a discussion forum where they can share examples of how they have prepared for university.

Take note

"Even though we encourage printed handouts, inevitably the dyslexic student will need to write notes at some point."

Taking accurate notes – from whatever source – is not only a key study skill, but also a life skill.

Notes can be made from written materials – textbooks, reports or articles, and from spoken sources – lectures, talks and seminars. Students with dyslexia need practice at dealing with both these situations. Suggest that students try the following activities, then report back on how successful they were.

Listen to someone – e.g. a lecture/talk

- Prepare in advance.
- Try to establish the structure of the talk or lecture.
- Fold one-third of the page lengthwise and leave it blank to enter key points later.
- Listen for clues, for example, repetition of points or emphasis.
- Remember anecdotes as a way of memorising.
- Keep thinking about the topic.

Take notes from written work

- Avoid simply noting down the words of the author. Translate into your own words.
- Do not begin taking notes too early: wait until the main points emerge.
- Assess whether or not a point is note-worthy before you write it.
- Try using spider diagrams and mind maps.

Other note taking strategies

- Use colour to separate topics or issues.
- Use highlighter pens to emphasise key points.
- Devise a simple shorthand.
- Keep the material well spaced.
- Add examples, if possible.
- Use headings and make lists.

Taking it further

It cannot be emphasised too strongly that organisation is the key to successful learning, whatever the activity. There is little point in taking notes if they cannot be easily accessed. There are several ways to store notes:

- loose-leaf paper in files
- on the computer
- in plastic boxes, on index cards
- in notebooks, with one book per topic.

The choice of storage will depend on the space available and student's preferences.

Dyslexia and
the overlap

Dyslexia and dysgraphia

"Dysgraphia can be difficult to cope with in secondary school, as there is usually so much writing. All teachers need to know about dysgraphia."

It is all too common for students in secondary school to have an aversion to writing. This is may be mistaken for laziness or assumed to be because they are dyslexic.

Teaching tip

In some cases the student may have difficulty with handwriting and with typing, and might be unable to use the laptop effectively. In this situation it is important that they have access to a scribe.

In this case the student will use their own idea(s), and the other person will do the writing. Care has to be taken to ensure that this does not affect self-esteem, so any partner or peer supporter has to be chosen with care.

It can be the case however that students are reluctant to write because they have an actual handwriting difficulty. In severe cases this is called dysgraphia. Although dysgraphia can occur on its own it is also commonly linked to dyslexia (or dyspraxia). Students who have both dyslexia and dysgraphia will need additional consideration.

Prepare a checklist with suggestions for accommodations as a whole-school resource for all staff. One of the most popular accommodations is the use of computers and specialised software, as these supports can help to overcome any demotivation that might arise as a result of dysgraphia. At secondary level there is little point in undertaking a handwriting programme, but rather the student should be supported to become proficient in the use of technology and have access to the laptop or iPad/tablet at all times.

The information sheet provided to the staff should include the following:

Characteristics of dysgraphia

- Letter inconsistencies
- Mixture of upper and lower case
- Irregular letter sizes and shapes
- Unfinished letters
- Often a reluctant writer
- Poor visual perception
- Poor fine motor skills

Points to consider

- Hand dominance
- Pencil grip
- Posture
- Paper position
- Pressure on paper
- Wrist movement
- Letter formation
- Left-to-right orientation
- Reversal of letters
- Spacing
- Letter size and formation consistency
- Style – joins in letters
- Speed
- Fatigue factors

Strategies and accommodations

- Provide blank copies of diagrams, charts and tables, which should indicate where responses should be inserted.
- Allow alternatives to handwritten responses, for example using a word processer or iPad.
- The student should not be penalised for poor presentation of work or misspellings.
- The student:
  - will need some guidelines for writing, and will require a framework for extended writing; model different types of writing in each subject
  - will need the most up-to-date software to ensure the editing features and spellchecker are appropriate for a student with dyslexia.
  - will need rest periods when extended writing is required.
  - should be permitted to use alternatives to writing such as charts, diagrams and pictorial representations.
  - will benefit from the use of digital voice recordings, to be transcribed at a later date.
- The use of mind mapping and bullet points as strategies to help with planning and structure will also be useful.

Bonus Idea ★

Using technology effectively

Students with dysgraphia can have difficulty with expressive writing perhaps due to lack of practice on account of their writing difficulties. Do encourage students to acquire competence in the keyboard as young as possible and it is a good idea in secondary school to make a list of all applications that can be used for students with dysgraphia and expressive writing and put this into a table form with a space for comments. This can be useful for the student but also for the parents. We are often asked for this type of information from parents.

Dyslexia and dyspraxia

"This is quite a common combination, and it can be extremely frustrating for the student"

Dyspraxia is a motor/coordination difficulty; it can affect fine motor activities such as pencil grip and gross motor activities such as movement and balance. The definition of dyspraxia, provided by the Dyspraxia Trust in England, is an 'impairment or immaturity in the organisation of movement which leads to associated problems with language, perception and thought'. (Dyspraxia Trust, 2001)

Taking it further

Read the case study below and make a list of the supports and accommodations you could offer.

Linda:

'I am 14. I have dyspraxia. I first found out when I was ten. The reason it was discovered was because I was seeing a counsellor for my behavioural problems. I was never able to finish my homework and then I got punishment, which was actually more written work and I could not do that either. I was eventually tested and it was discovered that I had dyspraxia.'

Look at the list below and, for your subject, note the particular tasks that can be challenging for each of the items in the list.

Students with dyspraxia can have difficulties with:

- gross motor skills – balance, coordination
- judging force in ball throwing
- balance/posture
- running, hopping and jumping
- tying laces
- kinaesthetic memory
- using two hands simultaneously
- spatial awareness and directional awareness
- copying and reading diagrams
- recalling detailed instructions
- reading and writing
- copying from the board
- using classroom equipment, e.g. rulers, compass, scissors
- following timetables
- finding their way round school, and also in some subjects such as Physical Education
- social skills.

Dyslexia and dyscalculia

"I find the working memory difficulties have a big impact on Maths, and there is often an overlap between dyslexia and dyscalculia."

Although dyslexia and dyscalculia do represent different aspects of learning and performance, there can be a clear overlap between the two.

There are so many factors in Maths such as working memory, sequencing, long-term memory and recall, focusing and processing speed that it is not surprising that quite a number of students with dyslexia can also have difficulties in Maths.

- Always write down the working out of a problem so the student can retrace their steps if necessary and keep the template within view.
- Make the teaching multisensory, with the use of age-appropriate concrete materials. For secondary students you can use playing cards, dominoes or a darts game.
- Remember that poorer short-term memory, slower writing speed and weaker knowledge of basic facts will mean tasks take longer.
- Mind map the terms and phrases that we use in connection with subtraction – minus, take away, how many fewer, how many less – and remember that sometimes the language can be counterintuitive.
- Give clear worked examples as posters around the room, and highlight signs etc. in colour.
- Plan backwards – write down the most difficult thing that you want students to know by the end of a unit and break it down into smaller skills.
- Use maths puzzles – have a puzzle of the week to challenge the class.

Teaching tip

Use visual devices to help students remember formulae – get them to visualise for example the > 'is greater than' and the < 'is less than' signs as open mouths waiting to devour the largest number.

Taking it further

There are many websites that can be helpful for Maths. One of the more recent ones includes a video by Steve Chinn (an internationally recognised Maths specialist): http://www.stevechinn.co.uk/about.html

www.mathsexplained.co.uk

Dyslexia and ADHD

"We need to respect the skills and the needs of children with ADHD, acknowledge the overlap with dyslexia and demystify ADHD."

It is not surprising that there is a strong view that an overlap exists between ADHD and dyslexia. Many of the cognitive attention processing mechanisms which children with ADHD seem to have difficulty with, such as short-term memory, sustained attention, processing speed and accuracy in copying, can also be noted in children with dyslexia.

Taking it further

Encourage staff to watch an informative and insightful video presentation on ADHD by UK expert Fintan O'Regan – the comments Fin makes in the presentation can be discussed afterwards with the staff – or better still, invite Fin to your school! http://www.dystalk.com/talks/53-what-is-adhd

The list below shows the various factors associated with specific learning difficulties, including dyslexia and ADHD, as well as dyspraxia and dyscalculia. Your task is to work out how these factors affect learning in your subject.

- Working memory difficulties
- Forgetfulness (long-term memory)
- Speech difficulty
- Reversal of letters
- Difficulty remembering letters/sequence of alphabet
- Confusing words which sound similar
- Difficulty with phonics
- Difficulty forming letters, colouring and copying
- Coordination difficulties e.g. bumping into tables and chairs
- Tasks which require fine motor skills, such as tying shoelaces
- Slow at reacting to some tasks
- Difficulty focusing on longer tasks
- Reluctance to go to school
- Signs of not enjoying school
- Reluctance to read
- Poor organisational skills.

Some final tips

Making your school dyslexia friendly

"Dealing with dyslexia is not one person's responsibility but is down to every member of the school staff."

There has been a drive to develop models of good practice in schools, showing that they consider the needs of all students with dyslexia. A school that succeeds is termed 'dyslexia friendly'.

A dyslexia friendly school values the role of staff development and recognises the needs and skills of students with dyslexia. The learning environment is supportive and caters for the diverse needs of all students.

The main reason for the success of dyslexia friendly schools is that they are proactive; they anticipate potential difficulties. In secondary schools teachers note how students with dyslexia might apply more global thinking solutions to a problem and develop more unusual and creative solutions.

Some suggestions for achieving dyslexia friendliness include:

- giving help discreetly to individuals
- providing additional time to complete a task
- providing printed handouts and summaries
- students working together in small groups
- grades and marking that show individual improvement so that they are meaningful for each individual student
- marking that is constructive
- work judged for content not spelling.

Prepare a worksheet for the staff in each department (this can be a whole-school activity or a departmental task). Divide the page into 'organisational strategies', 'note taking' and 'project work'. Staff can use this to make notes on progress.

Developing a communication system for parents

"If there is any one factor that can mean the difference between success and failure, it is communication between home and school."

It is important that parents can easily communicate with the school.

This means that the school should have a system in place to promote effective communication with parents. Constructive communication is the key to a successful outcome. If communication between home and school breaks down the student may receive conflicting and confusing messages in relation to their dyslexia, and this can be detrimental.

Communication can be in the form of a home/ school notebook that can detail the work done that day or week at school, and how the parents may follow this up at home. Or there might be a more sophisticated email system, or a combination.

Naturally personal communication is preferable, and parents and teachers should make contact as early as possible in the school term. The aim is that parents should be informed partners with the school and assist in supporting their son or daughter both emotionally and educationally, together with the school.

Ask the staff to contribute to a teacher/parent liaison system for dyslexia. What areas should you look out for, and what might you need to develop? (Think about the balance between home and school, providing a safe place and building students' self-esteem.)

Once completed you should pilot it with parents and evaluate its success.

Taking it further

You can ask the parents themselves what kind of communication they would like, and ask them to share any anxieties they may harbour about their child with the school.

Emotional literacy

"This is something that all schools must explicitly take on board – too often it is left to chance."

Emotional literacy relates to how 'well' students are emotionally, and the level of emotional competence they have in different situations.

Taking it further

This exercise can be done with the entire staff – divide them into groups and ask them to comment on the following factors and show how they can impact on emotional literacy. The idea is to recognise the features that concern all students, and specifically students with dyslexia.

Comment on:

• self-awareness
• motivation
• empathy
• social competence

and their potetial impact on emotional literacy.

Dyslexia can put the student under a great deal of pressure; in many cases the level of emotional literacy may be low and in need of attention. The checklist below can help.

• Does the student show signs of stress?
• Can the student be left to work independently?
• Can the student persist with a task or do they require monitoring?
• Can they only work for short periods?
• Does the student require constant reassurance?
• Is the student aware of the needs of others?

There are many other questions you can add to this, but these are some core issues that relate to emotional literacy. Try the following activity with the students.

• Divide the students into four groups and allocate each group one of the four emotion groups – happiness, anger, fear and sadness.
• Ask each group to discuss how that emotion shows itself in the classroom and school.
• Ask each group to consider how these emotions may impact on learning and behaviour – what things are easily managed and what may throw up disagreements and perhaps some stress.

The whole-group discussion after this is important; ensure everyone gets an opportunity to speak. Try to highlight the issue of diversity – at the end of it the students with dyslexia should feel no different from any other the other students; everyone has fears.

Getting lost around school

"Time management is an important factor in studying – it is important to use time effectively and know where to go and when. Even after years at a school this can be a problem for some students."

To be able to use time effectively students need to know where to finds things around the school.

They usually receive an orientation when they first arrive at a school, but some students with dyslexia still get lost even when they have been at the school for years. These students will need a strategy to help them get around the school more easily.

The problem is that when this happens and they get lost, it can easily be misconstrued as a form of deviant behaviour, which of course it isn't. It is a good idea to help these students develop a strategy that they can use in other walks of life, and even when they leave school.

A good activity to help with this would be to use a colour-coded map. The students can use the London tube map as an example – maybe a bad example – because it is very crowded. They can look at this as a starting point and indicate how they would like their own map of the school designed – perhaps they can make it better than the London tube map!

They can use different colours for different subject blocks, and they need to remember to make a clear colour code.

Taking it further

We mentioned the London tube map earlier (see Idea 34); students could try to design their own London tube map the way they would like it. They can use an existing one as a template. This can be good practice at doing this type of activity, and of course the tube map may well be useful later on.

Using technology across the curriculum

"As a teacher, I have seen how motivational the use of ICT can be for many students with dyslexia. Increased confidence, improved output and speed of work as well as a measure of enjoyment are just some of the advantages." (Dr Fiona Lyon, 2015)

Materials and teaching approaches for learners with dyslexia can be enriched through the use of computer programs.

Teaching tip

Select one computer program you are aware of, and note the advantages and disadvantages of that program. How, and in what circumstances, might you use this program?

There are a number of companies that specialise in software for learners with dyslexia. One such company is iANSYST Ltd (www.dyslexic.com). It provides a full range of text-to-speech software using the more advanced RealSpeak® voices, which are a significant improvement on previous versions, with a much more human-sounding voice. Such software can be very helpful for proofreading, as it is easier to hear mistakes than to see them and it can help to identify if any words are in the wrong place.

The TextHelp® range is highly recommended. TextHelp Type and Touch 4.0 has integrated speech output for PC or Mac, and includes the TextHelp spellchecker, which has been specifically developed for use by learners with dyslexia. Other computer support includes the Quicktionary Reading Pen, which transfers words from the page to the LCD display when they are scanned by the pen. The reading pen also speaks the words and can define the word when requested.

Taking it further

Get the students to make their own Wheel of Apps. They should insert the apps they use and say how they find them helpful.

There are also other popular programmes that help to organise information, such as Inspiration, for the 11-plus age range, which is also suitable for adults. These help to develop ideas and concepts, with examples of concept maps and templates that incorporate a range of subject areas such as languages, arts, science and social studies.

R-E-M software also produces computer materials specifically designed to help with dyslexia, and has produced a catalogue specifically for dyslexia (www.r-e-m.co.uk).

The CALL, which is based in and associated with the University of Edinburgh, has an open-access Resource Library of specialist books, journals, videos and multimedia materials. It can also provide advice on which version of the Spellmaster range is most appropriate for your needs. (http://www.callscotland.org.uk/about-us/our-services/information-and-advice/)

iPad apps

Many iPad apps are available to support learners with reading and writing difficulties. The Call Centre has developed an innovative Wheel of Apps, which attempts to identify relevant apps and categorise them according to some of the difficulties faced by people with dyslexia. It was originally published as an A3 poster, but works equally well as an A4 leaflet. Links on the electronic version are clickable, taking you to information about the individual apps on the iTunes site for the UK. (http://www.callscotland.org.uk/downloads/posters-and-leaflets/ipad-apps-for-learners-with-dyslexia/)

See also the Dyslexia Scotland magazine *Dyslexia Voices* edition on technology: http://www.dyslexiascotland.org.uk

Stress-proof the student and the teacher

"A stress-free school is a successful school — for all!"

It is extremely important that school should be as stress free as possible — in our experience it usually is, but sometimes it is difficult to judge the level of stress some students experience.

This is particularly important for students with dyslexia, as they can often hide their anxieties. There is a wide range of reasons why learners with dyslexia can experience stress. Some children are more vulnerable to stress than others, and trigger factors can be different in different students.

School is a social institution but some students find it difficult to fit in. This can make them socially isolated and can be a chronic source of unhappiness for many.

School can also be a competitive institution. This is okay to an extent as it can stretch students to achieve, but at the same time it can demoralise students who have difficulty in meeting expectations.

There has been much written about bullying, and many sources of support exist — e.g. anti-bullying networks. The potential for bullying needs to be monitored and action taken.

Unrealistic expectations are often the main cause of failure in school for students with dyslexia. The key to managing expectations relates to ensuring the task is differentiated to ensure that the student experiences success.

Show a list of potential stress points to the staff. Get them to add others and note underneath each point what they as a department can do to prevent or minimise their impact.

Glossary

ADHD – children with ADHD (attention difficulties with hyperactivity) will have a short attention span and tend to work on a number of different tasks at the same time. They will be easily distracted and may have difficulty settling in some classrooms, particularly if there are a number of competing distractions. It is also possible for some children to have Attention difficulties without hyperactivity. (This is referred to as ADD.)

Auditory discrimination – many children with SpLD can have difficulties with auditory discrimination. This refers to the difficulties in identifying specific sounds and in distinguishing these sounds from other similar sounds. This can be associated with the phonological difficulties experienced by children with dyslexia. Hearing loss or partial and intermittent hearing loss can also be associated with auditory discrimination.

Cognitive – this refers to the learning and thinking process. It is the process that describes how learners take in information and how they retain and understand the information.

Decoding – this refers to the reading processing, and specifically to the breaking down of words into the individual sounds

Differentiation – this is the process of adapting materials and teaching to suit a range of learner abilities and levels of attainment. Usually differentiation refers to the task, the teaching, the resources and the assessment. Each of these areas can be differentiated to suit the needs of individuals or groups of learners.

Dyscalculia – this describes children and adults who have difficulties in numeracy. This could be due to difficulties in computation of numbers, remembering numbers or reading the instructions associated with number problems.

Dysgraphia – this is difficulties in handwriting. Some dyspraxic and dyslexic children may also show signs of dysgraphia. Children with dysgraphia will benefit from using lined paper, as they will have visual/spatial problems and they may have an awkward pencil grip.

Dyslexia – this refers to difficulties in accessing print, but also other factors such as memory, processing speed, sequencing, directions, syntax, spelling and written work can also be challenging. Children with dyslexia often have phonological difficulties, which results in poor word attack skills.

Dyslexia friendly – this refers to the complete learning experience of the child. It includes how materials are presented, how the student is taught and assessed and the degree of awareness of dyslexia among teaching staff and management.

Dyspraxia – this refers to children and adults with coordination difficulties. It can also be described as developmental coordination disorder (DCD).

Emotional literacy – this refers to the extent to which children are aware of emotions and feelings; their own, but particularly those of others.

Information processing – this is a process that describes how children and adults learn new information. It is usually described as a cycle – input, cognition and output. Often children with dyslexia can have difficulties at all the stages of information processing.

Learned helplessness – this refers to the cycle of failure that some children may experience, particularly if they have repeated failures at the same task. The extent of this failure is reinforced by subsequent failures and it becomes a learned response to a task. Many children with dyslexia can experience learned helplessness with reading as they have repeated failures when they are engaged in this type of activity.

Learning styles – this can describe the learner's preferences for learning, which can be using visual, auditory, kinaesthetic or tactile stimuli, but it can also relate to environmental preferences such as sound, the use of music when learning, preferences for time of day and working in pairs, groups or individually. There is a lot of literature on learning styles but it is still seen as quite controversial, very likely because there are hundreds of different instruments – all of which claim to measure learning styles – and many learners can in fact adapt to different types of learning situations and environments. Nevertheless it is a useful concept to apply in the classroom, particularly for children with learning disabilities, as when using learning styles it is more possible to identify their strengths and use these in preparing materials and in teaching.

Long-term memory – this is used to recall information that has been learned and needs to be recalled for a purpose. Many children with dyslexia can have difficulty with long-term memory as they have not organised the information they have learned; recalling it can be challenging as they may not have enough cues to assist with recall. Study skills programmes can help with long-term memory.

Metacognition – this is the process of thinking about thinking; that is, being aware of how one learns and how a problem was solved. It is a process-focused approach and one that is necessary for effective and efficient learning. Many students with dyslexia have poor metacognitive awareness because they are unsure of the process of learning. For that reason study skills programmes can be useful.

Multiple intelligences – first developed by Howard Gardner in the early eighties in his book *Frames of Mind*, this idea turns the conventional view of intelligence on its head. Gardner provides insights into eight intelligences and shows how the educational and the social and emotional needs of all children can be catered for through the use of these intelligences. Traditionally intelligence has been equated with school success, but often this focuses predominantly on the verbal and language aspects of performance. Gardner's model is broader than that, which indicates that the traditional view of intelligence may be restrictive.

Multisensory – this refers to the use of a range of modalities in learning. In this context multisensory usually refers to the use of visual, auditory, kinaesthetic and tactile learning. It is generally accepted that students with dyslexia need a multisensory approach that utilises all of these modalities.

Neurological – this refers to brain-associated factors (this could be brain structure); that is, the different components of the brain or brain processing and how these interact with each other. The research into dyslexia shows that both brain structure and brain processing factors are implicated.

Paired reading – this involves the child and the teacher (or parent) reading aloud at the same time.

Peer tutoring – this is when two or more children work together and try to learn from each other. It may also be the case that an older, more proficient learner is working with a younger, less accomplished learner – the younger one is the tutee and the older the tutor.

Phonological awareness – this refers to the process of becoming familiar with the letter sounds and letter combinations that make the sounds in reading print. There are 44 sounds in the English language, and some are very similar-sounding. This can be confusing and challenging for children with dyslexia; they often get the sounds confused or have difficulty retaining and recognising them when reading, or in speech.

Reciprocal reading – the aim is to encourage the child to check their own comprehension. Small units of text are presented and the teacher reads aloud first and summarises what has been read. The purpose is for the teacher to model the read-aloud and think-aloud process and to encourage the child to self-question to actively obtain meaning from the text.

Scaffolding – this refers to the idea that specialised instructional supports need to be in place in order to best facilitate learning when students are first introduced to a new subject. Scaffolding techniques can include displaying graphics, activating prior knowledge, modelling an activity beforehand, and introducing motivational techniques to stimulate student interest.

Scanning – this refers to the process involved when attempting to locate a particular word or piece of information on a page.

Skimming – this refers to the process of reading by focusing on the key words only.

Specific learning difficulties (SpLD) – this refers to the range of difficulties of a specific nature such as reading, coordination, spelling, handwriting and number work. There are quite a number of specific learning difficulties, and they can be seen as being distinct from general learning difficulties. In the latter case children with general learning difficulties usually find most areas of the curriculum challenging and they may have a lower level of comprehension than children with specific learning difficulties.

TextHelp® – commercially available software to help with spelling, writing and reading comprehension. New versions have many additional features and are suitable for both children and adults.

Transition – in relation to education, transition usually means moving from one stage, school or environment to another; it is most commonly used in relation to transition from primary to secondary school, and from secondary school to post-schooling options.

Overlearning – this refers to repeating the same task, or piece of learning, a number of times to help the learner consolidate the information.

Working memory – this is the first stage in short-term memory. It involves holding information in short-term store and carrying out a processing activity simultaneously. This can be solving a problem, reading instructions or merely walking around. Students with dyslexia often experience difficulties with working memory and have difficulty in holding a number of different pieces of information at the same time.

References

Askew, M. (2013) New curriculum, new futures: learning mathematics for life. Keynote Presentation Victoria State Government: Education and Training Conference 28th September 2013, Melbourne, Australia

Chinn, S. (2015) Maths Explained www.mathsexplained.co.uk

Diniz and Reed (2001) Issues in Inclusion : In L. Peer and G. Reid (Eds.) Dyslexia and Successful inclusion in the secondary school. London David Fulton Publishers.

Diniz, F. (2002) Interview for audio E 801: *Difficulties in Literacy Development*. Milton Keynes, Open University.

Freeman, D. (2010) Once Upon a Pose: A Guide to Yoga Adventure Stories for Children. Trafford Publishing. North America and International www.trafford.com

Henderson, A. Came, F., Brough, M. (2003) Working with Dyscalculia: recognizing dyscalculia and overcoming barriers in Maths. Learning Works International Ltd. www.learning-works.org.uk

Howlett, C. A. (2001) Dyslexia and Biology in L. Peer and G. Reid (eds.) Dyslexia – Successful Inclusion in the Secondary School. David Fulton Publishers. London.

Knightly, K. (2014) article in BDA Music Committee Newsletter Number 5, February 2014.

Overy, K. (2008) Music and Dyslexia: A Positive Approach. Wiley, Chichester, UK

Reid, G. (2016) Dyslexia: A Practitioners Handbook 5th edition, Wiley-Blackwell.

Wearmouth, J. (2001) Inclusion – Changing the Variables in L. Peer and G. Reid (eds.) Dyslexia – Successful Inclusion in the Secondary School. David Fulton Publishers. London

Wearmouth, J., Solar, J. and Reid, G. (2003) Meeting Difficulties in Literacy Development: research, policy and practice. London, Routledge Falmer

West, T. G. (1997) In the Mind's Eye: Visual Thinkers, Gifted People with Learning Difficulties, Computer Images and the Ironies of Creativity. Prometheus Books, Buffalo, NY, USA.

Websites

www.drgavinreid.com

www.redroseschool.co.uk

www.dysguise.com

www.arkellcentre.org.uk/

www.dyslexiaaction.co.uk

www.allspecialkids.org

www.interdys.org

http://www.dyslexicadvantage.org/

www.das.org.sg

www.icepe.ie

www.dyslexiascotland.org.uk

http://www.senbooks.co.uk

http://thedyslexiabookshop.com/

http://www.tompousse.fr/fiche.php?livre=43&collection=100-idees

www.funtrack.com.au/

http://www.dyslexiaassociation.org.au

http://www.speldvic.org.au

http://www.speld.org.nz/

http://www.dyslexiafoundation.org.nz/

www.learning-works.org.uk

www.texthelp.com

www.globaleducationalconsultants.com

www.crossboweducation.com

www.dyslexic.com

www.dyslexia-international.org

www.barringtonstoke.co.uk/